SAME BAG, DIFFERENT BUNK

My Life Inside American Hostels

I0530858

ZACK REED

Same Bag, Different Bunk: My Life Inside American Hostels

Published by This Could Be Good
Copyright © 2025 Zack Reed
Cover Design by Erika Scipione

ISBN: 979-8-9999833-0-5 (Paperback)
ISBN: 979-8-9999833-1-2 (eBook)

Manufactured in the United States of America
Published 2025

The names and identifying characteristics of several people described in this book have changed.

TCBGMEDIA.COM

Special Thanks to Bobby Dyer & Gayle Burgundy

Hostel: an establishment that provides inexpensive food and lodging for a specific group of people, such as students, workers, or travelers.

That is the dictionary definition. However, after reading this book, you will see that hostels are much more than that. Still, you will find that this is only one person's perspective on the hostel industry in America, a mere glimpse at some of the strange, interesting, and otherwise enlightening things that it can offer someone like me, who is willing to stick around long enough and put up with some of the bumps that may occur along the way.

It was not my intention to write this book, nor to spend more than a year cycling through American hostels, living out of the same bag and swapping bunks as they became available, but life has a strange, serendipitous way of working out. As for how it all got to that point, where there was enough material for a book, perhaps the best place to start is with that awful train ride from Austin to Los Angeles.

Table of Contents

An Unexpected Delay - *San Antonio, TX*

I felt their eyes needling me with every movement as they sat in the lower car, several gawking as I shoved Josh off the train. He tumbled, nearly tripping over himself on his way across onto the platform. He stumbled through a crowd of pedestrians before finding somewhere to lean.

The place was downtown San Antonio. The hour was late, somewhere around 11 pm. And there were still thirty-some hours of rail time ahead of us. An impossible thought to fathom as I watched several strangers approach my friend, who had his head slung over a railing, a dribble of chunky spit spewing from his mouth. Others, who had been walking by but did not dare to approach, merely stopped to stare.

Of the few that came up to me, quietly asking if my friend was alright, I tried to deflect the attention the best I could.

"He'll be fine, thank you," I said, avoiding eye contact. "He's just...unwell. Eaten something rotten, I'm afraid."

It hit me suddenly that there was still a sloppy mess to clean up, back on the train. I ran back to the upper car where we had been sitting. First foot up the stairs, and I could smell the sour vapor of Josh's stomach acid, the faint, smoky aroma of the Mezal lingering ever so slightly. Hands trembling, I found the nearest paper towel dispenser, pulled a wad, and got down on my hands and knees, using the small bottle of water I had with me to splash the surface before holding my breath and wiping away the clumps of Josh's vomit from the floor.

I returned to the platform, where Josh stood hunched over with his head slung and spit bubbling from his lips. Before reaching my friend, I was intercepted by a man in uniform. I saw him coming out of the side of my eye, and stopped walking as he flagged me down.

"Is your friend OK?" asked the man. It appeared he was one of the main conductors: this was going to go one of two ways.

"Yes," I said, hesitantly. "Just had a little too much to drink."

The man sighed. "It happens," he said, lowering his voice. "But, if your friend throws up on the train, you guys are *both* off."

"Yes, sir. Understood," I said, quickly nodding. "*If* he throws up on the train, we're off. Got it."

The man's tone suddenly changed. He became sympathetic, almost to the point of apologizing for having to address the situation.

"It's not about *me*," said the conductor. "I just can't deal with the *other* passengers. It would be chaos, I'm telling you. He cannot throw up on that train."

"Got it," I replied. "Well...do we at least have some time?"

The conductor glanced down at his watch.

"This train takes off at 2:30. With or without you," he said, before walking away, leaving me to wonder what else could go wrong before then.

I turned to look at Josh. He was still slouched over the railing, spewing vomit in short, violent bursts, fading in and out. More people were watching us by now, a few nosey pedestrians whispering as they passed by.

I put my hand on Josh's back and leaned in to tell him that we might have just caught a break.

"Just drink the water," I said, lifting a large bottle to his face. A dribble of spit hung from his lip as he stared at the ground, defeated. He looked like hell, as if he had just picked a fight with the wrong person and lost.

"I need to go lay down," murmured Josh a moment later, swiveling his head to look up at me. His eyes were bloodshot.

"OK, but right now you need to stay here," I said. "And drink this."

Normally kind and easy-going, Josh became suddenly irritated by me and my efforts to control him.

"I'm going to lay down," Josh said angrily, and then staggered off to the train.

The train car was still empty. All the other passengers seemed to have had the same idea: to explore the city, once the conductor had announced the four-hour layover, once we rolled into San Antonio.

Josh found our original seats and dropped down next to the window. I took the seat next to him and settled in.

"Is he OK?" came a soft voice next to me. I looked over to see a woman sitting in the opposite row. She was African American, roughly my age, but a mother with a toddler in her lap. She looked concerned as her eyes found my friend.

"He will be," I said. "Thank you."

The woman gave me a half-smile and then returned to soothing her toddler. Another conductor made her way down the aisle, checking the tickets above each empty seat. The conductor's eyes found Josh, who was fidgeting in his seat, groaning as he tried to get comfortable.

The conductor must have given him a disapproving look, because my friend turned to her and said, "fuck you, bitch."

The woman stopped in her tracks, astounded by my friend's unprovoked behavior.

"*Excuse me?*"

"He didn't mean it," I quickly said, putting a hand on Josh's chest. The conductor stood there, glaring at us. There was a moment of tension, but then she pressed her lips together, clicked her tongue, and continued walking down the aisle before disappearing through a set of sliding doors. Maybe, I thought, as the doors snapped shut, she was too tired to do anything about it, or at least had heard worse in her time, and these two clowns weren't worth the hassle.

While Josh spent the next hour fading in and out of sleep, I made small talk with the woman next to us. Her name was Shareen, and it just so happened that we were originally from the same city. Shareen had come down south to visit family and was slowly making her way west before circling back to the Midwest.

At one point, Josh snapped out of his sleep and stood up. He began trying to crawl over me on his way to the aisle.

"Let's go, bro," he said. "Let's go see San Antonio."

"Absolutely not," I said, yanking him back down. "*Sit down.*"

My friend struggled before finally freeing himself. Sneering, he looked down at me, laughing at my failed efforts to control him. This side of Josh I had only seen once before, and it was only so ugly because of how contrary it was to his normal self. The switch had been flipped now, though, and there was no turning back. And it was my fault.

Suddenly, Shareen stepped in. She spoke softly to Josh, as if she were giving her son instructions.

"Sweetheart, why don't you sit down. Get some rest, baby. You've had a long day. You need to sleep."

Josh looked down at Shareen, and gradually, his expression began to change. Something in her voice seemed to strike a chord in him, and my friend became suddenly relaxed, under total control of Shareen as if he had just been hypnotized.

"That's right, sit down, sweetheart. You need to relax," Shareen continued to say. Just like that, Josh shut his eyes and dropped into his seat. A few moments later, he was asleep.

I looked over at Shareen, astonished. She only smiled back and returned her attention to her toddler.

Once I saw that Josh was knocked out, I crept out into the aisle, taking my bag with me, and found the nearest bathroom. I had to dispose of the evidence, just in case. The sight of the bottle itself was nauseating as I lifted it out, staring at the familiar bottle of Mezcal before sending it spiraling down the sink. Gulping a few times on its way down the drain, the smoky liquor disappeared.

I looked into the mirror, blinking preposterously as the moment sank in. The realization of what had just happened finally hit me, and I felt a confused anger.

But I wasn't upset with Josh, not for chugging his entire share of the bottle that I had brought for us within the first 30 minutes of a 30-some hour trek across the desert, nor was I mad about his complete change in behavior and unruliness. No, I was upset with myself for thinking that bringing the liquor with us was necessary in the first place.

When I got back to my seat, the empty bottle stuffed between a few pairs of socks and underwear, I saw that Shareen had a keen eye on Josh as she bounced her son on her lap. We smiled at one another as I sat down in one of the empty seats behind Josh, eventually drifting off to sleep.

All of a sudden, I was being throttled awake by a hand on my arm. It was Shareen, tugging my sleeve. She pointed frantically at Josh as he stumbled down the aisle, with his hand over his mouth. I leapt from my seat and slipped in front of him, pulling his shirt over his mouth to cover the impending spray.

"No, no. Not here!" I hissed, through gritted teeth, maneuvering so that I could be the one to catch the spillage, which came splattering onto the train floor and onto my shirt.

Just as I had before, I tossed Josh down the train stairs and onto the platform, only on this run, slicing my hand open on the way off. Josh stumbled back to the same section of railing and hung his head over it, hurling onto the pavement. As I watched my friend from afar, I felt a strange release in tension. In a way, I felt weightless, realizing that the game was up.

As I approached Josh, I noticed he seemed to be coming to. His dark, heavy eyelids slowly opened as he hung his head over the railing. Josh groaned in disgust when he saw the mess on his shirt, as if realizing for the first time what had just happened.

I placed a hand on his back, rubbing gently as he spat out a bit more onto the platform.

"Wait here," I said quietly. "I'm going to go get our stuff."

When I returned, Josh had his head in his hands, leaning against the railing. Seeing his bags and mine over my shoulder only affirmed our defeat. First, I handed him a jug of water, and then began rifling through his bag, as well as mine, pulling out a fresh pair of clothes.

"Take your shirt off," I told him, and then did the same. Josh peeled off his foul-smelling shirt and then watched silently as I went to throw it into the trash, along with my own.

A myriad of thoughts came flooding through my mind as I walked back to where my friend stood on the platform, his face marred with disdain as he stared down at his bags.

"So we have a few options," I said to Josh. "We can look for a hotel in San Antonio and take the first train back to Austin tomorrow."

My friend nodded grimly.

"Maybe there's a bus that would be cheaper, I'm not sure. Or…we can call a car, which, I'm sure, would be expensive. But maybe not…" I paused. "And then, there's the cheapest option." Josh looked at me inquisitively. "We could always sleep *here* and wait for the next train out, which…I wouldn't necessarily say it's the best choice. But it's an option."

Josh remained silent for a moment.

"Just go, bro. Get back on the train," he said finally. "Go to LA. I'll get back to Austin on my own. This is your vacation."

I stared at Josh. That was one option I didn't even stop to consider. For a moment, the temptation rose, but then it fleeted. I wasn't going to leave him, especially since it was because of *my* harebrained idea that the two of us were in this mess in the first place.

"No, man. We're in this together. We'll get back to Austin somehow."

Josh pursed his lips and nodded. We stood in silence for a moment before I spoke up.

"*Or*…we can get back on the train, and just *see what happens*." I looked around. "Maybe no one saw you throw up. Maybe we can still get to LA."

Josh looked at me and began laughing.

We took our seats next to Shareen and her son. She gave me a cool, assuring look from across the seat. Like last time, Josh was quick to curl up into a ball and get right to sleep. Things felt somewhat back to normal, even if at any moment it could all go to hell.

But as the moment steadied, I began to breathe deeply, and eventually, I fell asleep. Perhaps an hour later, murmuring voices and shuffling feet had found their way back to the cabin, stirring me awake. With a weary eye, I looked down at my phone to check the time.

"Please take your seats. The train will be departing momentarily," came a voice from the speaker overhead. Then a pair of sliding doors at the end of the cabin flung open. Two men emerged and began walking down the aisle toward us. My heart began to beat furiously against the sides of my chest.

At that moment, the night felt as if it was either going to implode on us or fade away into the darkness of the cold, vast desert.

I shut my eyes and tried to feign a deep state of sleep as the two men made their way toward us. Their feet stopped suddenly, and a voice called out, "There he is! That's him, that's the one!"

I shut my eyes even tighter, using every ounce of energy to appear asleep, completely unaware of the situation. The moment lasted for what seemed to be an eternity as the men stood next to us. I expected my arm to be seized and to be escorted off the train.

But the moment passed, and the voices grew distant. Millimeter by millimeter, I let one eye slip back open, watching two shadows disappear as the cabin door opened again.

Frantically, I leaned forward, looking for Josh, who was curled up in a ball in the row ahead of me, his face buried in his sweatshirt.

I sat back, and, not a moment later, the train jerked forward. It began slowly tugging away from the platform, one heaving throw at a time. Hammering still against the sides of my chest, my heart felt like it was about to explode. I could not understand what was happening.

Then, all of a sudden, the train came to a stop. The cabin door behind me flung open again, and the two men returned to where Josh and I were sitting. I felt their presence as they loomed over us, but it was Shareen's voice that I heard first.

"They didn't do anything wrong," she pleaded. There was an exchange between Shareen and the conductors, which I could not fully make out.

"But they didn't throw up *on* the train," Shareen said. "Give them a break, would you?"

Their conversation continued for another moment before finally going quiet. The cabin door slid open again and then closed. A few seconds later, the train began to tug slowly before picking up great steam and disappearing into the night.

It felt like a dream, waking up in my seat as the darkness of night was slowly peeled away from the ground, and the world outside my window found definition again. I found Josh in the observatory car around 10 o'clock. He could not believe the story when I told him, leaving out certain parts to spare his embarrassment. Of course, he was ashamed of what he had said, what he had done, how it could have been so much worse. But all that could have happened needn't be discussed. It was obvious that we had caught a break—perhaps one we didn't deserve—but also that our little blunder would do us both some good for some reflection.

Los Angeles was just another stop on the map for me, but it had long been on Josh's bucket list of US cities to visit. As someone who moved from the Middle East and assimilated into the American lifestyle, but had not yet officially become a citizen, for Josh, Los Angeles was still the land of dreams, beautiful people, and pristine beaches.

My friend, however, would have less than 24 hours to see everything that he could before hopping on a plane back to Texas to get back to work. What made at least part of Josh's hopes to explore the city possible was that Mike, an old friend of mine, had come out West to chase the Hollywood dream and was still living there, so he offered to pick us up and show us around the city for the day.

When Josh left, I still hadn't decided when I would be leaving LA, as I had been booking all my stops with last-minute one-way tickets. The longer I spent catching up with Mike, the more I came around to the idea of sticking around, especially since he and his roommate were so accommodating.

"Stay as long as you'd like," Mike told me. So, I did.

The two of us were getting coffee at a small, funky cafe down the road from his apartment in Culver City, a few days later, when Mike dropped it on me.

"So I was thinking," he said, once we found a table outside. "I've got to take this job in New York next month, but I really don't want to leave LA. It'd be a shame to have to get rid of the apartment, since it's in a good location and actually cheap for LA. So, what would you say about maybe renting out my room, while I'm gone?"

"Funny," I said. "I was actually thinking the same thing. Though I wasn't sure if it was even an option."

Mike was relieved. "No, bro, that's the *best* option, actually. Because if I rent it to some random person, who knows what will happen if I hate New York and want to come back. This way, it can be flexible for both of us, given your situation and all."

"Sure," I said, without thinking any more about it. "I'll take it."

When Mike dropped me off at the airport later that week, he went out of his way to say how grateful he was and how this could be the best thing for both of us.

"Maybe you'll love LA, and I won't want to leave New York," he said.

Flash forward a month later. The car was packed for California. The plan was simple: I was to arrive in Los Angeles on the first of the month with money in hand, ready to take the keys from Mike's roommate, since Mike would already be in New York.

My brother and I had set out to run some errands the morning before we were to set out on the road, to grab the last little odds and ends for the trip. He and I were sitting in the parking lot of a chain department store when I decided to send Mike a text, wishing him well on his early endeavors to New York City. There was a short delay, and then my phone lit up with a few text messages from Mike.

Shit, I forgot to call you, sorry bro.
The apartment got flooded. We all had to move out.
The one guy who was actually on the lease wasn't willing to keep it going, since he hasn't lived there since...

More messages came rolling in, but I stopped reading them and set the phone down. Turning to my brother, the only thing I could do was laugh. My brother shot me a confounded smirk. I took a deep breath and then held up my phone to read Mike's messages.

"Wow," said my brother. "This sort of shit just happens to you, doesn't it?"

He had a point, but that was beside the point.

"Ok," I said. "Well, what do I do now?"

Befuddlement came over my brother. "What? Are you kidding me? Let's go, bro."

I gave him an uneasy glance.

"Oh, come on," said my brother. "If you don't find anything, go work at a hostel or something. You'll figure it out."

1

The Aftermath

I took my brother's advice because not only was he usually right when it came to this sort of thing, but I had at least experienced staying in hostels for a stretch, and, while many of those experiences were positive, there were a few I would rather have back. But what I would quickly come to find out was that staying at a hostel is one thing. Working as a volunteer is an *entirely* different experience. It can be—if you are open to it, or at a place in life where such a thing is even possible—life-changing.

Frankly, I was indifferent to the idea of moving to LA in the first place; the opportunity merely fell into my lap, and so when it came time to decide whether to stay there or go somewhere like San Diego, I opted for the latter and sent out several messages to hostels looking for help in San Diego. Within just a few days, I heard back from one that was located downtown and was offered the position to volunteer for a month at the hostel. The agreement was to sign up for that first month and then see where things went.

While I did not end up packing my bags again for several months, it became quite clear to me along the way that I had stumbled into something rather special and unique, and perhaps had I chosen a different hostel, or decided to do such a thing at a different point in my life, I would not have thought it so necessary to stay as long as I did.

What I would go on to experience in my time working at that hostel in San Diego, moreover, was indelible on me and would go on to shape my outlook on life and the world as I knew it.

Before that treacherous train ride with Josh, I had traveled extensively throughout the United States. I had seen most of what I needed to see and was lucky enough to meet people from all over the country with different stories and outlooks. I had yet, however, to truly be exposed to the *rest* of the world, as I had been to my own fellow Americans.

Unbeknownst to me at the time, the first hostel I chose would kick that door open for me, and, as I found out, I would not even need to venture outside of the building for something interesting, attractive, or profound to come my way.

Make no mistake about it, hosteling for long stretches of time is a flawed lifestyle, and there are more than a few compromises to be made along the way. There are aspects to this lifestyle that are not always glamorous, nor is every moment romantic or epiphanic. However, there is an underlying aspect that makes it all worthwhile, which, for me, was the exposure to new cultures and interesting characters. Perhaps most importantly, it was a place where I could almost always be doing something new with someone different all the time.

The range of individuals that one might encounter at one is, moreover, a large part of what makes the industry so unique, and perhaps, just the same, curiously misunderstood.

Perhaps if I didn't have to find last-minute accommodations after my friend's apartment in Los Angeles flooded, I would have never wound up working at one, and quite likely would have not understood them as I do now.

Landing at the right one likely had something to do with it, because there had already been established a culture that was welcoming and brimming with energy and optimism. It was, however, a bit of an adjustment at first, and I recall being a bit rattled when I walked into the staff dorm for the first time by the realization that *this* was what I had signed myself up for.

But when I started to meet others casually piecing their lives together with one-way tickets and instant-noodle budgets, I realized that perhaps I wasn't so crazy, after all, for working a job just to make enough money to spend it in half the time, somewhere far more interesting. In many of the people around me, both fellow volunteers and overnight guests, I came to see that same desire and unrelenting itch to explore. Many of these individuals spoke without a hint of regret about the decision to adopt this way of living; some said they would not change it for anything. In fact, the opposite, to them, sounded a bit crazy, especially since many of them had tried it already and would wave their hand at it dismissively.

And yet, as much as this book is about *my* personal experiences and the collection of months that I spent living out of the same bag, trading out door keys and fresh towels as they were handed over, it's about the people that shaped the journey, and how I found them in the most unsuspecting of places: American hostels.

2

A Brief Introduction to the Hostel Industry in America

With four other friends and a few thousand dollars between them, Jim Kennett purchased a condemned building in Bandon, Oregon, in 1978. The reason for purchasing the building was to create something for the community, but when it came down to deciding on something that could serve the community *and* make money, he and his friends chose a hostel. The idea of starting one was planted in Jim's head several years before, when he and his girlfriend were traveling through parts of Canada and the US, staying mostly in hostels along the way.

At the time of the Bandon purchase, Jim was coming off a few-year stint as a caretaker for an 180-acre ranch on the Oregon Coast, and wanted to do something of his own, even if, at the time, he only expected his time with the hostel to last a short while.

Flash forward a few years, and he and his friends brought the building to life with renovations and built it out into a hostel. It became popular and revered by travelers, but as time went on, each of the partners in the business went their separate ways and were bought out. Suddenly, Jim was the last one left.

"I figured from there, I probably wouldn't last more than two years," said Jim. "And here I am, forty-seven years later, still running hostels."

Since starting that first endeavor in Bandon, Jim has gone on to hold panels, consult other hostel owners, and serve as the President of the North American Hostel Association (NAHA). A lot has changed since the 70s when Jim started his unexpected life-long career, and the hostel industry—while it still relies on the same principles of providing travelers with affordable accommodations and creating community through shared spaces—is no different. Back when Jim and his friends started the hostel, they ran, like most other hostels, on a chore system. This meant that each morning, a guest was tasked with tackling some minor chore or cleaning project within the hostel. A small price to pay, considering the cost of a bed at that time was anywhere between $3 and $5. Holding people accountable, as is a challenge for any business owner, was, however, not as difficult as it might sound.

"Things were simple, back then. People would grab a broom and do their chore," said Jim. It worked as well as it did because the steady mix of backpackers meant that the work could be split evenly, and it helped that not everyone viewed the chores the same way.

"The Europeans didn't mind cleaning a toilet, whereas that's the *last thing* Americans wanted to do," laughed Jim.

Just in case, though, he and his other staff members would go through the hostel after each round of checkouts and ensure that the tasks were completed as they were assigned. While sometimes an extra sweep or swab of the toilets was necessary, Jim saw that the simple task of cleaning the space brought people together.

"I will say that (the experience) builds a community," he said. "It made the people feel like they were a part of a place they were staying. They weren't just visitors."

While the chore system has been largely phased out in hostels around the United States, that same sense of community can still be cultivated in the volunteer program, which has otherwise supplanted the chore system by enlisting volunteers at the hostel to do the daily chores, in trade for their accommodations. Therein, however, lies a gray area, which is shirked entirely by some hostel owners but utilized by others.

For Jim, as the operation in Bandon grew and profits increased, the need for unpaid workers diminished; instead, he opted to pay his staff to do the work of a volunteer. Part of the evolution of the industry, as Jim saw, was also that the expectations of travelers had changed.

"Nowadays, hostels have to be so well-equipped. People are paying $50 or $60 for that, to have someone come and clean up after you, and to have amenities like free wifi," he said. Back in the day, guests were simply glad to have an alarm clock, hair dryer, or courtesy phone available. In contrast, today, the range of amenities offered in hostels is often much greater, partly reflecting the increase in the price of a bed in a shared dorm or private room.

For as much as has changed in the world since starting his first hostel in Bandon, Jim acknowledged similar threads in the travelers that have come through his hostels over the years. People are still naturally a bit shy when it comes to being placed in a room full of strangers. They typically need an icebreaker, some way to get the conversation going, and find things to connect over. That can be as simple as having a common travel destination, fluency in the same language, or a similar sport of choice.

Activities like walking tours, surf sessions, pub crawls, or game nights are often a good way for people to connect at hostels, as they require some degree of socialization, but as Jim pointed out, connections can occur over something so primitive and basic as cooking dinner side by side. Two backpackers from opposite sides of the globe might find themselves sharing the same stove one night and then pal up for the rest of their trip.

Cultivating the right vibe and creating spaces where those connections can occur effortlessly and organically—making people comfortable with the uncomfortable—then, is part of the art of hosteling. An art that many hostel owners around the world try to refine each day.

The number of hostels in the United States alone has grown tremendously since Jim first got his start, but he and hostel owners around the US continue to face an uphill battle of diluting a stigma around their industry that has been largely miscast, and will do so as long as the concept remains foreign to many American travelers, simply because they have never stayed in one.

But as Jim, and so many others—whether that be hostel owners, volunteers, or simply guests—have witnessed through their experiences at hostels, it only takes a small window of exposure to see that the thing we might be reluctant or hesitant to engage with could be the thing that makes a lasting impression upon our lives, and perhaps even change it for good.

Although there's a myriad of individuals around the world who could expound on the beauty of hosteling or wax poetic about how this unique way of living changed the trajectory of not only their career path but also their personal lives, it comes to little surprise when I still hear skepticism in someone's voice about American hostels, or listen to someone who lived in a certain town admit that their community initially pushed back on the idea of a hostel being opened there.

The main crux of this unfortunate misconception that many Americans have about hostels is because of a lack of exposure; simply not enough of them have experienced them in the same way that international backpackers have—many have never set foot in one.

Hostels remain, then, something of a mystery to so many Americans, particularly those who have not traveled much. Take a friend of mine from back home, for example, who, after finding a hostel to work at in San Diego, told me that he was concerned for me once I had explained the volunteer program at the hostel and how the hostel would be my home for the foreseeable future.

"What, do you want to wake up with a kidney cut out?" he laughed.

While it was made in jest, my friend's half-cocked question underscored exactly what is wrong with many Americans' perception of hostels and why the industry has long struggled to gain a real footing in this country, as it has in countless others around the world. There are walls that stand in the way, walls that, unfortunately, prevent someone like my friend from ever seeing what's on the other side. Those walls, then, become only fortified and emboldened as the narrative continues to be driven by more slander, more propaganda, and more cheap Hollywood flicks about the 'horrors' and 'frights' of staying at hostels.

But whether or not one chooses to peek around the corner of that wall or to take a sledgehammer to it and start to chip away at its foundation, there are different ways to shift the narrative on what staying at a hostel can be like; for the sake of this book, I opted to take the sledgehammer route.

3

A few of the Things I've Found Behind That Wall

My first overnight shift as a volunteer seems like an appropriate place to slowly unravel many of the thoughts and memories that occurred during my time staying and living in hostels.

It was my first time working the graveyard shift, and, before even clocking in, I had an odd feeling something strange was going to happen.

I was scrubbing a toilet bowl when, around 2 am, my phone rang. It was a friend of mine. He was at the house around the corner, which was also part of the hostel, watching a movie in the lounge.

"Hey, what's up?"

"Hey, bro, uhh…you better come back here," said my friend Chris. He lowered his voice. "Some shit is about to go down."

Immediately, I assumed the worst, and although that strange gut feeling portended something weird happening, I had not at all expected what was about to unfold.

"Fuck. Alright, I'll be right there."

Up to that point, the most difficult encounters came with someone who was trying to book a bed for the night, but did not seem like the type of individual that I would feel comfortable spending the night in a room with, so they had to be asked to leave. These were rare, but not totally uncommon, being that the hostel was located downtown San Diego.

Chris might have liked to bust my chops, but I could tell by his voice that he wasn't joking. I set down the cleaning bucket and hurried around the corner to the other house.

Chris was leaning in the door of the reception area, standing alongside a petite foreign girl with a large digital camera around her neck. The girl's appearance and timid mannerisms made the situation even more confusing, considering *she* was the reason I was called over.

"So, what's going on?" I asked them.

Chris sighed and then explained that he had tried to help the girl, but he had gotten the sense that she wanted a refund for something, but he was not able to give her one since he was not on shift, so he called me. But there was more to the story.

"She told me..." Chris hesitated. "There was a man, outside, with *a machine gun.*"

"I'm sorry?" I turned to the girl. "You said he was *outside?*"

"Yes," answered the girl, urgently nodding her head.

Chris and I looked at one another. He turned his head, trying to hide his laughter. I walked to the door and poked my head outside, but the streets were just as empty as they had been just a moment ago. Not even the rev of an engine could be heard in the distance.

"I'm sorry, miss. But there's no one out there with a machine gun. I just came from outside and I did not see anything like that," I said, now looking at Chris for help. There was a moment of silence from the girl as she stood there, staring at us.

Chris turned to the girl with a straight face and said, "OK, so then if there *is* a man outside with a machine gun, why would you not want to stay here, *inside*, where it's safe? With us? No one is going to hurt you here."

The girl only stared blankly back at him. There was a sort of vacancy in her eyes, stirring in my gut that something *was* off. But as for her outlandish claims about a man outside with a machine gun, I could not, in good conscience, give her money back for no good reason, especially since the hour was so late and it would be soon time to check out.

Finally, I said to the girl, "You can hang out in the lounge until the morning, if you'd like. I'll be working reception until four o'clock, so someone will be here throughout most of the night. The next person starts their shift at six."

Shaking her head, the girl finally gave up and then walked out the front door with her expensive camera around her neck. I was a bit taken aback, given that San Diego was not necessarily what one would consider to be a small city, and for even an American, not the safest place to be walking around alone in the dead of night.

Through one of the windows in the reception area, I watched in bewilderment as the girl stood idly on the street corner, gazing off into the distance. A lot of different things ran through my head as I watched her eventually turn a corner and disappear. I wanted to have a good reason for the girl's strange behavior, but had none. It appeared, at that moment, that this would not be the last strange incident I would experience at the hostel.

The strange and otherwise impressionable characters, however, who may come through any hostel on any given day, are what make the experience of staying in them so fascinating, even though that sometimes entails managing the ones who are a nuisance or at first annoying.

It would have been easy to be annoyed by 'One Kool Kat' ('OKK'), who was quite a bit older than I was and many of the other guests at the hostel that week. But she was just the same as any other curious backpacker, wanting to see as much as she possibly could on her visit, so each morning, 'OKK' would have a car booked to take her across town. To the museum. To the botanical gardens. To Balboa Park. To Ocean Beach. One time, all the way up to Carlsbad. By my loose calculations, her car rides far exceeded the cost of her stay at the hostel.

'OKK' got her nickname only because she let one of the staff use her phone to call her a car for the following morning. The staff member happened to notice that 'OneKoolKat' was part of her old Hotmail email address, and so, naturally, the name stuck. She was rather a nuisance, herself, needing all sorts of trivial things at all hours of the day. 'OKK' was the type of guest, moreover, that, every time a staff member saw her coming, they would turn around and find something to do or look for a room to hide in.

'OKK' happened to find me one day while I was outside on the patio of the hostel, tucked in a corner, rolling a joint to spark after taking an important work call. Seeing that I was alone, but still occupied, 'OKK' strolled over to where I was sitting, grinning with a full beer in her hand and a bag of weed in her front pocket, and then she pulled up a chair. We smiled at one another and said our pleasantries, and then she grabbed the bag of weed and proceeded to retrieve a pipe from her pocket, in the meantime explaining to me just about everything she had done during the day.

I listened casually while continuing to roll the joint on the table in front of us, but then all of a sudden, as if she were at home, lounging on the sofa, 'OKK' propped her bare feet up on the table and began to get comfortable.

"Agh...my bunions are killing me," she groaned as she stretched her toes out, right next to the pile of weed I had laid out. 'OKK' lit her bowl, wiggling her toes in front of me, as if nothing was at all amiss. Trying to remain cool and calm, whilst steadily moving my raw goods away from her bare, bunion-laced feet, I asked her what some of her favorite sights in San Diego had been so far.

"Oh, it's hard to choose just one," she said.

'OKK' had loved her time in San Diego and was sad to be leaving tomorrow.

"But this has been pretty cool," she continued. "And they have these in every city?"

"Most," I said. "At least, the bigger ones. Though sometimes they're in remote areas."

"Hm," said 'OKK', lancing a layer of foam from her beer. "I had no idea. I should look into that next time I'm traveling."

We talked about San Diego for a little while longer, until I finally looked down at the time and told 'OKK' that I *did* have a pressing matter to get to, and would need some privacy for the call that would be coming in any moment.

'OKK' was quick to pick up her belongings and salute farewell before torching the rest of her bowl and strolling away with her half-finished beer in hand. The woman might have been needy, yes, and her silly requests made for a few inside jokes amongst the staff, but that 'One Kool Kat', I realized, was a lot like the rest of us, trying to have a good time and looking for someone to talk to.

The turnstile of faces becomes, however, a blessing and a curse, and they can make it seem like time is either flying by or standing completely still. With the way that door constantly spins, it's easy to look past someone or forget them soon after they're gone, but just as well, it only takes one person to stop everything, and maybe even change your life for good.

It was not long after the 'man with the machine gun' and 'One Kool Kat' that I was having a conversation with my friend Burak from Turkey out on the patio one night after a BBQ, and he said something to that effect.

"You never know who you're going to meet that will change your life," said Burak.

That specific line sticks out to me, not only because my friend didn't have the best English, but knew how to articulate *that*, but also because, just a week later, I met a few travelers who would, in fact, change my life.

Having already been at the hostel for a few weeks, my one-month agreement as a volunteer at the hostel was coming to a close; still, I was conflicted about whether to stay or go. I hadn't fallen in love with the city, nor had I found any particular reason to stick around; San Diego was a fine city, but I had the travel bug, and there was nothing there that truly compelled me to stay beyond that one month — until Camila and

Vince, a pair of backpackers from Italy, arrived at the hostel.

Camila had just been brought on as a new volunteer at the hostel, and it was within our first few minutes of conversation on the patio that I felt a connection, some sort of intrinsic energy, to her and Vince. It was a feeling that I could not put into words, other than it was just a feeling that I not only should stay, but that I *needed* to stay.

And so, like many of the other individuals in this book, my one-month agreement turned into several, and that first conversation sparked what became a lasting friendship with two people I would have never met, had I never decided to do the hostel volunteer program. Camila, too, extended her time as a volunteer at the hostel until the very last day that her visa would allow, because of, I can only presume, a feeling.

Over the next several months, we had the good fortune of having a few other backpackers from different countries come to do the volunteer program, and it was through the work itself, as well as the many meals prepared and shared, plus countless late nights out and days spent cruising around town together, that a unique bond was established, which would last well beyond our time at the hostel together.

So when Steve Best, one of the partners at ITH Hostels, said to me, as we sat down for an interview in San Diego, that it was something he had to learn the hard way—how to say goodbye but also how to reset, in order to remain open and willing to embrace the next individual as they walked through the door—I could only nod, and say that I understood, remembering the tears that were shed on the day each of those backpackers I worked with had to go their separate ways. But I also understood—which Steve later said—that there was a beauty in that, even if it came with its share of pain.

It doesn't require sharing meals, cleaning sinks and toilets together, or living in the same room together for weeks at a time to learn about people and what makes them tick; sometimes it occurs through a conversation that may start with a simple, "So, where are you from?"

It may seem formulaic or banal, but if there is ever a question as to how to break the ice with someone in a place like this—especially if the idea of socializing with strangers in new spaces seems intimidating or does not come naturally to you—it starts with that one question. For me, personally, that single exchange of information has led to several friendships that have far outlasted the time spent in one particular city or area, adding a degree of permanence to something that was inherently fleeting.

At the same time, it's not always about the people you meet at hostels but rather what you may learn about yourself along the way. In the collection of months that I spent bouncing around various hostels, sometimes working as a volunteer while others focusing primarily on this book, the conversations I had with other volunteers at the hostel—current or previous—would often segue into that one thought: self-growth.

The amount of personal growth that one can experience in a place like this, moreover, can be hard to quantify, as it does not happen overnight, nor is it necessarily tangible or visible from the outside. But that process, as I have seen and experienced firsthand, is a slow transformation, and it may not even register as having occurred until one looks back and thinks about how they viewed the world and themselves as a part of it before they arrived at the doorstep of that one hostel.

Camila, when she came back to San Diego a year later, elucidated that very thought when we met for drinks at one of our old haunts downtown. As we sat at that familiar bar, in San Diego's bustling Gaslamp District, the table crammed with empty margaritas and plates of tacos, Camilla opened up about where she was, but also how it was, largely, a byproduct of where she had been.

"It's weird. So much has changed since I left. *I've* changed," said Camilla, looking around. "But I didn't realize that, and just how much this place shaped me, until I left, and went back to Italy. That's when I realized, I grew a lot here."

"Sure, I know what you mean," I said. "Sometimes I feel like I've become a different person two or three times over since we both showed up to work at the hostel. It's hard to put into words sometimes."

Camilla looked over the table at me and smiled, not saying anything but nodding as she took a drink from her margarita. It was funny being back, considering how much *had* happened in the previous year, and how that single decision to stay at the hostel for longer than a month had altered the trajectory of my life in such a way that I would not have been able to comprehend at the time. Though so many of the faces at the bar and the hostel had swapped out, some of the familiar ones were still hanging around, and a few made a point to stop by the table and say hello.

The bar was as busy as it had always been, with people lining up out the door and putting their names down for the beer pong tournament. Partly because of the latter, but mostly because of their cheap specials, *this* became the spot for us, one of our usual stops where we brought other travelers and international backpackers to experience a taste of the American nightlife. A lot of late nights protracted into early mornings, and they often started on the patio of the bar, rolling cigarettes and spliffs as we watched the people go by.

Now that we were a year older, and in different places in our lives, but also, in a lot of ways still the same, it was serendipitous to see that the things that brought us here in the first place had found a way to bring us back. And it started, at least for myself, with the decision to stay, that first night she and Vince showed up, because of that *feeling*, as inexplicable yet intrinsic as it may have been.

That feeling which gave spark to a fuse that was long buried inside of me—to experience a lot of everything, sometimes all at once—is what kept me hanging on, perhaps longer than was necessary, but long enough to see that it was, after all, just what I needed.

4

People Just Being People

D oing this long enough, you're sure to meet someone who is wildly different from the person you met the day before. If you choose to listen, or at least carefully observe, you might just see that while each traveler is different, there are shades of that person in someone else you had previously met or known in the past, perhaps even at that same hostel.

It's part of what makes the human study side of it so fascinating, because, in just about any hostel in the world, you're going to encounter the ones who talk too much and want you to know everywhere they've been and what it took to get there. At the same time, that person might be quick to fill the space with trivial facts or travel tales but will be hesitant to explain *why* they are where they are, and even more reluctant to add how long they plan to be there.

Although they are not always one and the same, there are those who might start off nice, but once they realize they have an angle, something to take, gain, or

41

even leverage, they become a different person. Perhaps then they'll pull out all the stops, which often means lying to you and, even more so, lying to themselves.

By and large, these individuals are not bad people, but along the way, perhaps they missed out on that *thing* that they were supposed to do in life, and then that regret, the underlying 'woe is me' outlook becomes something that they weaponize to either defend themselves or manipulate a situation. Since the hostel and its sanctity rely on the energies and efforts of the people that occupy them, having someone who is ostensibly always looking for an angle to exploit or someone new to ensnare in their own false reality— whether those efforts are clandestine or not—can become a parasite that gets stronger and more difficult to remedy with each day that passes.

Identifying these individuals before they are able to sink their teeth into a space becomes easier with time, but it is an inexact science to be sure, and perhaps the worst thing that a staff member or hostel owner can do, when such a character exposes themselves for what they are, is to let that individual entrench themselves deeper into the place and indoctrinate the innocent guests who have come for quite the opposite experience.

While there will eventually be someone else out there like them to replace them, sooner or later, allowing these individuals to be the anchor that slows down the operation or even brings it to a halt can jeopardize the experience for many other people in the building.

Since hostels rely so heavily on people, it is only natural, then, that a less-than-savory character or two will make their way through, and often want to stay. Finding ways to kindly ask them to leave is never easy, but such a thing can be necessary, since the ship must be steady and no one person must attempt to become bigger than the operation. And while there might be energy vampires or charlatans looming in the shadows, there are also those who want to teach you a thing or two about life.

The older hostel guests, as I have found, can be the ones who add the most perspective to something as deep as religion or as simple as gratitude for the space that the two of you presently share.

I often think of the old Irish woman who came to Santa Barbara and sat at the table with nearly a dozen noisy twenty-something backpackers, all pounding shots before a bar crawl. As the young travelers hooted and hollered, the woman kept shaking her head and smiling, saying how it took her back to her youth when she backpacked through Europe and used hostels to save money while exploring several different countries.

"I'm lucky," said the woman. "My co-workers wanted to stay at a hotel. They found a fancy one down the road. But, this is *much* better." She grinned, looking up at the clock above the kitchen door. "I'll bet they're already in bed, watching the tele, thinking about what they'll do tomorrow."

While the main demographic for hostels is, in fact, travelers in their twenties and thirties, it was often the older guests that I found myself gravitating toward. Whether that was on a deeper level, like the fellow I met who had such a fascination with numerical sequences that he found them playing so heavily into the outcome of his life that he became highly superstitious about them, or whether that was on the surface like the old German motorcyclist who, like my grandfather, smelled like a pack of wet cigarettes but spoke perplexingly in broken English about the socioeconomic conditions in the United States and why they were part of the reason he remained a Communist, the range of conversations and characters encountered in a place like this can feel overwhelming, given how small the facility itself might actually be, and how soon one will eventually be gone.

Being shut off by someone's appearance, however, or assuming that the two of you have nothing in common, because of that glaring age gap or sharp language barrier, may severely hamper the experience, since one of the many reasons for booking a hostel, as opposed to a hotel suite or someone's cozy apartment, *is* the sharing of spaces, things, ideas.

That can involve sharing something as simple as a crowded oven, a laundry machine, or a crammed sofa, or it can encompass something as deep and profound as a conversation or an intimate connection.

Throughout that process, it has become just as clear to me that, while we all have our own thoughts, idiosyncrasies, or stances on how things *should* be, one thing is true: people are people.

Having spent more than a year living out of the same bag while cycling through several hostels, it's difficult to pick out a single moment as being more impressionable than another; rather, when reflecting on each of the nights out, mornings around the kitchen table, or afternoons spent exploring a new area with someone from another country, what stands out the most *is* the people, not the places.

The places, as ever-changing and often beautiful as they have been at times, often become secondary to what is being experienced, whether that is a sign of affection, a six-pack of beer, a travel hack, or even the bones of a new language. So, as they have been with me, the profoundness of such moments and the people who help create them, I can only assume, is the catalyst behind someone choosing to stay at a hostel rather than a more private or comfortable set of accommodations.

As for what has kept me around, I can only speak for myself, but for the other characters in this book, the beauty of the *people* became all but echoed through our conversations. Like myself, several of the individuals who were interviewed or otherwise made their way into this story, coming to work or even staying at a hostel, were more of an accident than an intentional decision.

For some, arriving at the doorstep of a hostel was because of a single suggestion by a friend or family member. Eric Faria, who first started working at ITH Hostels in San Diego in 2012, shared how his initial decision to try a hostel forever changed his life.

Having come to the United States to take English lessons as a young Brazilian, Eric realized rather quickly that sitting in a classroom with a bunch of other non-English speakers just wasn't cutting it. After months of studying, he struggled to truly grasp the language and was not learning it as quickly as he had hoped. That's when Eric's friend recommended he stay at a hostel, since there were several in San Diego.

"The first day I showed up, I met the receptionist and within five minutes of being there, I had more conversations in English than I had in my entire month at school," said Eric. "It was that first impression for me that made me realize: I need to be here. These are my people."

As several other foreign travelers I had met along the way had similarly stressed, spending extensive time in a hostel proved more fruitful and informative than any English class they had to pay to attend. The usage of language, moreover, is amplified in hostels, because of how necessary it is for the everyday things that come with living in a common place. That can be as simple as asking what time breakfast is, or as complicated as asking for directions to the nearest grocery store.

Sometimes you get lucky, like Eric, and there might be other travelers from your country in the hostel at the same time, allowing you to share your native tongue and feel more at ease as you assimilate into a new environment while trying to pick up a new language. But what refines the skill is practice, and since communication is one of the main fibers of communal living, a hostel can be an ideal place to start.

"Hostels are the best environment if you want to learn a new language. I doubt there is a faster way to learn a language than there is by being in a hostel," said Eric.

Deciding to work at the hostel not only allowed him to pick up English as a second language quickly, but it also became a launching pad for Eric's future endeavors, even if he had no idea what sort of relationships or professional connections it would offer him when he first signed up for the volunteer program. Eric's website, Worldpackers.com, came to life sometime later, and a few of the individuals he worked with during his time in San Diego became key members in the company. Over time, Worldpackers has become one of the most popular search engines for finding volunteer opportunities in hostels around the globe, with Eric and his co-founder still running the show.

It can happen unexpectedly, as it did for Eric, me, and several individuals in this book. For others, deciding to sign up to work at a hostel might be calculated into their bigger plans, seen as a springboard or way to soak up as much industry knowledge as possible before starting one of their own. Dave Cook is just one example of someone who started out as a guest before becoming a volunteer, scrubbing the outdoor grill, cleaning toilets, and sweeping floors, only to, years later, become an entrepreneur and open a hostel of his own.

Dave, like Eric, underwent a deep personal transformation because he decided to work at a hostel. But, for Dave, it was not obvious at first. He had shown up to the original ITH hostel in San Diego down on his luck, having driven all the way out to California looking for work and to start fresh, but had come up short and was running out of options. After doing some digging on the internet, Dave's mother booked him a room at the hostel, and although he had no idea what to expect, that single decision to stay changed his life for good. With tears in his eyes, Dave recalled showing up to the hostel to check in and being immediately embraced by one of ITH's co-founders, and how that single interaction left a deep imprint on his life.

"I had already shed the person I was with that hug," said Dave. "Stepping outside your comfort zone even further isn't hard after that."

Flash forward six years, Dave went back to the East Coast and opened up the Barn Door Hostel and Campground in Rumney, New Hampshire. Things coming full circle for him is one thing he keeps in mind while running his business, having been brought up under some of the most successful independent hostel owners in the US.

"It's interesting to see the other side of the coin today. *I* was that lost person. And now I see those lost people walk through. It's kind of rewarding. That's my main motivation for running this place in the first place. To allow others to do and feel that moment I had that first morning," said Dave.

While they are designed to provide safe, affordable accommodations for travelers, every hostel is different. Each one, with all of its moving parts, becomes a rather complex ecosystem made up of a variety of different factors, and so no two establishments feel the same, even if they're run by the same company.

A poorly run operation can feel like a runaway freight train, whereas a good one can seem like an anomaly, with people not wanting to leave and forgoing their own travel plans to instead work for a month or two at a time as a hostel volunteer, just to get more of *it*. The industry is littered with examples of the former—downright uncommendable establishments that deceptively call themselves a 'hostel'—and there could be whole chapters written on all of the liars and the otherwise undesirables who are looking to drift more than they are to go forward. But the latter, the hostels that *do* operate the correct way, functioning as they are supposed to, are what have helped the industry in the United States grow as much as it has, even if American hostel owners continue to fight the gross and otherwise unfounded stereotypes that prevent many of their own citizens from ever setting foot in one.

With so many to choose from, it's natural that someone might choose to stay at a hostel that is merely passable and provides them the most basic set of accommodations, which may dampen their outlook on what they *can* be and prevent that person from ever trying one again. Admittedly, the first American hostel I ever stayed at was stale and not remarkable in any particular way. But I met a few backpackers there who helped show me that it's not always about the amenities or having a nice, soft mattress, and that inspired me to book more hostels as I continued traveling the US.

The individuals inside each one largely dictate how someone might experience a hostel. However, just as with any customer-based business, the experience can also be significantly influenced by the building in which they operate. I've stayed at a few that felt like they were just thrown together—with walls so thin that every noise was amplified through the night, or putrid water pressure in the showers, hardly what one could consider 'hot'—which makes sense given how challenging it can be, as a proprietor, to find the right location at the right price, one that suits the specific needs of a hostel with the adequate infrastructure or does not need to be bulldozed entirely and built anew. I've been to others that felt rather like a repurposed doctor's office, with stiff overhead lighting, rigid mattresses, and mysteriously stained carpets, which have made me feel like I was being punished for something, rather than being a guest in someone's place of business.

But those sorts of hostels are few and far between —and even though they do exist, experiencing the ones that don't come with any bells and whistles, or where sleep is hard to come by and the staleness is palpable, may rather force one to find ways to spend their time *outside* the hostel and explore the place they came to see in the first place.

There are many ways to experience a hostel. They can be, as specified in the dictionary, an affordable place to stay for travelers, students, etc.. Hostels can, on the other hand, become a portal to places that would otherwise be too far out of reach, impossible to access without someone *from there* showing you what it's all about. Explaining their people, *and* yours.

The more you ask of them, your fellow bunkmate or breakfast goer who has come from somewhere far away and is filled with excitement to see the States, the more they might be willing to share. It becomes reciprocal, if one is so open and willing to engage with that curious individual; and I have discovered, only by being in a place like this, how so many foreigners seem to covet *'the American way'* with an insatiable appetite, some even noting how relaxed *we* are, and social, compared to other countries, where it might be customary to keep groups or confide only in their immediate company.

I've listened to women chuckle about how men in their country use different tactics to sweep them off their barstools, amazed at how easy it is here to get a drink, even if there's no other reason to take it other than that it's *free*. Still dancing and having a good time, because that's all that they came to do anyway.

I've been told, just as well, how 'clubbing' can mean different things in different countries, and in the same breath, how Americans actually *don't* know how to party, only for the rest of the room to fly into a heated debate about what that even means.

But it's that effortless exchange of cultures and new outlooks on the world that make the experience of staying at one so enriching, and hearing those stories might suddenly catapult that country toward the top of the list, which seems to be growing with every week that passes. And perhaps what is so special about that is that you do not even have to step foot off the property for those revelations to be realized, or that new door to be opened.

5

How Easy it can be to get Carried Away

It was one of my more forgettable moments at the hostel. Having established the routine of leading our weekly tour to a nearby bar for their taco specials, it was only natural that I was the one who led the group of backpackers out that Tuesday night in San Diego. Of the guests staying at the hostel that night, only two joined, and I gave a distinct heads up, on our walk to the bar, that, once we all ate, they would be on their own that night. I would not be coming back with the group, as I normally did, so the message was to plan accordingly.

But even going into the night, I had a suspicion that the night could end up spiraling on me, given that one of my old childhood friends was in town for the night on a work trip, and that he was as bad an influence on me as my friend Chris, who was also working at the hostel that night. My friend from back home and his co-workers had flown into San Diego for a few days to attend a work conference that was being held just a few blocks away from the bar where we were eating, so it was an easy place for us to meet up and start the night.

Where it all unraveled, from there, has a lot to do with *how* we all chose to spend the next twelve hours. My friend and his group arrived right as we were finishing dinner, and after seeing off the hostel guests and saying goodnight, I split from the group and found my friend and his colleagues huddled around the bar. My friend and I elbowed one another aside as we decided on who was paying for the first round. And then the second, third, fourth...

By the time the fifth tequila shot went down, I was ready to leave. Once the notion came up of us leaving, however, my friend and his co-workers vehemently opposed the idea.

"It's pretty jumpin' here," said one of them. "Is everywhere else in Gaslamp like this?"

"Probably, but maybe not on a Tuesday."

"Let's just stay here," said one of the guys, watching with a smile as groups of girls danced on table tops; the others were in awe, seeing the servers come prancing out in their lingerie as they began giving bottle service. We hung out at the bar for a while until Chris showed up. He just finished his shift and was ready for a drink when he showed up. Chris immediately ordered tequila shots for my friend and me, plus two for himself. That led to another round, and another. Eventually, six became seven and then, somehow, seven became ten.

As the liquor crept in, the place became even more packed, with more people crowding the dance floor and others lining up to play beer pong. Some of my friend's co-workers were still hanging around; others had turned in early, saying on their way out that the morning would come all too soon.

"Yeah," said my friend, looking down at his watch begrudgingly. "We did start drinking pretty early at the baseball game. I think this will be the last one for me."

Once my friend and his co-workers said goodbye, Chris and I signed up to play a round of beer pong. But for whatever reason, we weren't very good and lost our first game.

"Let's get the hell out of here," said Chris. "I'll get us one more round, but then let's hit up Whiskey John's for a nightcap. I like that place."

Whereas the bar we had just left was packed out, Whiskey John's was completely empty aside from a few staff members chatting in the corner. Chris and I settled up at the desolate bar, and he put down a twenty-dollar bill.

"Two shots of Don," said Chris. The bartender gave us a careful glance, nodding as she went to retrieve a bottle from below the bar. She took his money from the bar and handed over two tall shots. Chris and I must have been distracted when she went to pour the drinks, because when we put the glasses to our lips, it was obvious that the tequila we ordered was not the one we received. It smelled like petrol and tasted even worse.

"Excuse me," I said, starting to feel my pulse quicken as the liquor stung my lips. I was more confounded than I was upset. "This...is not what we ordered."

The bartender tilted her head and looked at us. "Yes, it is," she said, and then turned away and began cleaning the bar.

"Actually, it's not," I said, raising my voice. I found myself holding back my laughter as I argued with her. "This is *not* Don. It tastes like you poured us rail tequila, actually."

The girl looked up from what she was doing and then said, indolently, "No, I poured you what you ordered."

By then, one of the bouncers had made his way over and began watching us argue with the bartender.

"Right, well, can we speak with a manager? Because this is not what we ordered. It's not even close."

"Is there a problem here?" said the bouncer, his eyes narrowing as he moved forward.

"Yeah, there is," laughed Chris. "You guys are trying to fuck with us. I ordered top shelf tequila, not this garbage. She poured us something that was *not* Don. It's much, much worse."

The bartender and the bouncer turned their backs to us momentarily, whispering to one another.

"She said she poured you what you ordered," said the bouncer, shrugging with a snide grin.

"OK, cool," I said. "Then why don't you pull up the security tapes and show us that *this* is what we ordered. Because I can assure you, it's *not* what we asked for. Y'all are trying to rip us off."

The bouncer merely stood there, his arms folded, and that same smug look on his face.

"Sorry, bro. We don't have security cameras here. The girl said she gave you what you ordered. That's that."

"I can't believe this! I don't know what kind of scam you guys are running here, but this is definitely not right. This place is terrible, no wonder it's empty," I exclaimed.

The bouncer just stood there, smirking at us as the bartender went about her business and continued wiping down the bar. Leaning against the bar coolly, the bouncer kept a close eye on us, waiting for the opportunity to toss us out.

"Fuck this, and fuck you guys," said Chris finally. "We're *never* coming back here, and we're going to tell all of our guests to never come here either. Y'all should be ashamed of yourselves."

Unflinched, the bouncer watched us, grinning cheekily as we got off our stools and stumbled out of the bar.

It took me a while to realize the next morning that my phone was missing. In a half-drunk, dazed state, I began tearing the bed apart, tossing my sheets and throwing pillows around as I frantically searched for my phone. Then that sinking realization hit me like a ton of bricks: you got hammered and lost your phone. *You idiot.* This was out of character for me; the phone was brand new, too, hardly a few weeks old. The nicest one I had ever owned.

I closed my eyes tight, my head throbbing and mouth shriveling up as I tried to hone in on *what* exactly it was that happened that night. Only shades of the night came back to me in spurts, and after piecing certain parts together, it became obvious: my phone was left at the bar, with the kind folks at Whiskey John's.

In a daze, I threw on some clothes, dug out my old backup phone that I brought on the road in case of emergencies, and stumbled out of the dorm room. The high morning sun was like a belt to the face as I busted out of the hostel doors and staggered toward the city center. My first stop was to the bar, naively hoping an honest individual returned a phone the night before.

"Sorry," said the lackadaisical hostess, hardly looking up from her service station as she shrugged. "No one here knows anything about a lost phone."

Though as I stood outside the bar, I couldn't help but feel like *something* was off. Then again, I had no choice *but* to believe her, being that I had no true recollection of what exactly happened the night before. Filled with shame, I walked to the nearest cell phone store to reactivate my old phone so that I could at least try to figure out what to do next.

Once it was up and running, the first person I called was my friend from out of town who had been at the bar with us earlier that night.

"Damn, bro. That sucks," said my friend, once I explained how the night had so unexpectedly gone off the rails. "It could have been worse, though," he added. "You could have ended up in Tijuana at the brothel like my two co-workers. One of them is still missing."

Without having to name the name, I knew *exactly* which brothel my friend's co-workers had gone to that night. Still, I had to ask what happened; I felt slightly better, knowing what he said was true: my night *could have* been worse.

"So," my friend started laughing, lowering his voice as he began retelling the story. "These two guys decided—after bar close—to get a cab down to Tijuana. Even though we had a meeting first thing in the morning. They found a brothel, did what they came to do, and then started planning how to get back. But one of the guys wasn't ready to go. He wanted to stay in Mexico, *at the brothel*. The other guy said, 'That's a terrible idea. There's no way in hell I'm doing that. I'm leaving. You need to come with me.' But the one guy refused, and finally he left him there, alone in Tijuana. But once the guy got in the cab, he realized he didn't have his passport."

"Oh no."

"*Yeah*," my friend chortled. "So, the cab driver gets him to the border, and once he finds out the guy doesn't have his passport, he tells him he needs $500 so he can get him across the border. Naturally, my co-worker is pissed off and starts arguing with the cabbie. But, of course, he realizes he has to pay; otherwise, he's not getting back into the States. So, he gave the driver all the cash he had, something like $300. Finally, around six a.m., he makes it back across the border and shows up at the hotel just in time for our first meeting."

"Wow, OK. *That's* bad," I said, once we both stopped laughing. "Just when I thought I had a rough night. But, wait. What happened to the other guy?"

My friend let out a nervous laugh. "Yeahh, so they actually don't know where he is at the moment. His wife tried calling him. So did our bosses. No one can find him. They sent someone from HR down to Tijuana this afternoon to go get him. He's *definitely* fired once they find him. The bosses are pretty pissed off right now at us, especially those guys. But, at the same time, they understand that the one guy made the right decision and at least *tried* to talk the one guy back into coming."

"That sounds terrible."

"*Yeah*," laughed my friend. "It's pretty fucked up, I'm not going to lie. This dude just totally went off the deep end. Now corporate's all up our asses, so we're all sort of being punished for last night. They said no one can go out again tonight. So I guess I'll see you when I see you."

As the week unfolded, both missing items showed up. Thanks to tracking technologies, my phone was located somewhere outside of the city a few days later, at a suburban residence, which happened to be owned by one of the kitchen crew from Whiskey John's (strange). As we sat outside the house, waiting for the phone to be brought out, the police officers were rather frank with me.

"You're lucky. This usually doesn't happen," they said, somewhat perplexedly.

"No...it doesn't," I said.

Before even speaking with the police and arranging a squad to meet me at the scene, I was offered by more than a few of my friends at the hostel, folks I had made good with in my short time there, to come along with me to the address where the phone was located, to confront the individual who stole it. They happily offered to be my muscle, if needed; at the very least, to be that extra bit of support for what was an uncertain and potentially dangerous situation, since there was no guarantee that showing up at some stranger's door and demanding my phone back would go smoothly. Even though I had no intention of taking them up on the offer, I was grateful for merely having the option.

It was a nice reminder knowing that even in a transient place, a space like that, I still had people in my corner, people who were willing to go to bat for me, even if the situation was largely my own fault. The phone was recovered without any issues, and when I got back to the hostel to show my friends, they leapt from their seats and celebrated my small victory.

As for the missing co-worker in Tijuana, he turned up, too. They found him the next morning, drinking whiskey out of the bottle in his underwear in a trashed hotel room in Mexico. Not only was he fired, but the guy had to pay the company back for the expenses on the trip. All things considered, I got off somewhat easy, but I took it as a real lesson to know when enough is enough.

6

L'Amore: That Thing

I f you're not careful, you could end up falling in love, and it will change your life completely. In a place like this, traditional paths can be completely thrown off course, even smashed to smithereens, often due to that one person sitting across the table at breakfast or out on the same bar crawl. I've heard, seen, and experienced how slippery the slope can be, how easy it is to get caught up in a good feeling and think it will never end. For some, it doesn't, and there are weddings and perhaps a few baby showers to follow.

Bobby Dyer was one of those people. One of the co-founders of ITH Hostels, Bobby, met his wife while working with her at one of the first ITH Hostels in San Diego, and, several years later, they started a family together. He spoke on what it is that brings people together and why the idea is so infectious from the start.

"Who *doesn't* like the idea of falling in love on vacation? It's exotic, meeting someone on a trip, especially a person from another country," said Bobby.

Love, it seems, is part of the reason that some travelers continue to stay in hostels, as opposed to hotels or other arrangements. In hostels, there can be a whole room full of potential matches on any given day, and from that, a world of possibilities.

As someone who has worked in hostels and witnessed two people fall in love in real time, it can be difficult not to envy the life of a nightly guest, longing for the luxury they have that you do not, which is simply having no obligation but the moment, and being able to recognize when it is necessary to stop or even change directions entirely due to a *feeling*. How it all may go from that point ranges immensely, but in a place like this, things can happen fast, and sometimes those heated flings turn into trips somewhere else, and from there, a new life.

Whether it prospers or not, that idea of love can also be as intoxicating as it is infuriating when you have to put a pin in it, for now. But from all the pain that can come from that, there's a beauty in having been able to have it in the first place. Ask around, and someone will eventually start to tell you about him, her —the one that got away. That person they *should have* chased, even if it would have meant putting certain things aside or others in jeopardy.

It never gets easier, seeing that person move on, or perhaps even watching them suddenly become more interested in the next interesting backpacker that walks through the door, since that is also part of the game.

And part of playing the game means knowing you could lose at any point.

Love: finding ways to say it or private spaces to make it can be tricky, given just how much of the space *is* communal and the experience temporary. Most hostels offer private rooms for rent—often couples will book them, even families reserve them from time to time, but the large majority of guests stay in shared dorms, which can create quite the pickle, especially when the place is full, because by the time you realize you need a private room, they're usually booked out.

Like privacy, sex is something humans inherently covet and enjoy. And when the need arises to satisfy the latter, and decisions have to be made or chances need to be taken, one's self-respect may need to be put aside, or a bit of forgiveness might be required at the end. Some travelers are quite successful when it comes to this part of the experience and take full advantage of always having new, exotic, and sometimes incredibly beautiful people coming through the hostel each day, even pulling off a quick shag with another guest without anyone else in the hostel knowing better. Others might fail because they are not crafty enough, or the timing simply doesn't line up. But one way or another, it usually gets figured out.

It's not always about sex or sparking some deeper connection with another traveler, but when it is, if you do not shoot your shot, it's almost certain that someone else will. And you'll be left on the sidelines, watching the game end in dramatic fashion. The agony of regret, however, is far more painful than any sting of rejection.

I suppose that's why some people don't mind taking as many swings as they possibly can. That goes for both sexes—people, especially in a place like this, will never stop being *people*. It just so happens that hostels bring people together in small spaces and require them to coexist with one another, at least in some capacity.

It was while working on this project, stopping off sometimes for days or weeks at a time at a certain hostel, depending on who was where, when, that I befriended a volunteer who was rather friendly with his fellow volunteers. So *friendly* that his behavior eventually caught the eye—and ire—of his superiors. My friend was not fired for being so amicable with the opposite sex; he was merely asked to move locations, as his bosses were simply trying to get ahead of something.

"It is one thing to hook up with one staff member, maybe two," the manager would say, pausing. "But, literally *every single one*?"

Something has to give, eventually. Allowing that sort of thing to happen will, at least eventually, invoke some chaos. Moments like this are why folks at the hostel would often joke about how the daily drama had all the makings of a reality television series, which held some weight. The people and their sometimes unrelenting desire to satisfy that certain *need* are as much a part of the fiber as sharing a freshly cooked meal or a useful travel hack around the breakfast table, and it has the most natural way of coming out, given the way the place operates.

But things can turn quickly inside of a hostel—a strong culture can carry a team for months, and it's just as susceptible to crumbling ostensibly overnight because of tangled emotions or messy personal affairs. Strong ties may suddenly become untangled because of an urge someone had to fulfill that desire with someone they knew would be gone soon, too. And by the time that person—the one who may have been pulling strings—has moved on, somewhere else or to another spot in town, the ramifications of what they've done have fully set in, and now it's up to someone *else* to put the pieces back together.

It's inevitable that emotions will get crossed in a place like this. Being so open and still interdependent, a hostel can feel like being in a fishbowl, where everything is seen, and even the smallest signals or signs of affection that do occur can feel incredibly magnified, especially if someone is watching, an admirer perhaps, who has just had their heart pulled out because of the ease at which their crush might carry off with someone else for a night, even if that is someone whom that person has just met and will be gone by tomorrow.

With so many interesting and adventurous people coming through the door each day, it's hard not to fall in love at least a few times over, even if you never find the time or right way to say it, and that idea of that person stays with you well beyond your time together at the hostel. You might get a kiss when it's all over or maybe even a promise that you'll see them again soon. You might even hold out hope that at some point along the way, perhaps at another fork in the road, you find one another, whether that is on your soil, theirs, or some complete far away country, because what called you there, seemed to have called them there, too, and so it doesn't feel so foolish to think that lightning could strike, again, even if you are uncertain as to where or even when.

Give someone enough time, and they'll tell you about love. Old or young, they'll open up to you about the *real* romance, the spicy affairs, the ones who made them almost give up hope on it entirely, the times they flew to another state or country on something of a whim, perhaps even leaving something of a life behind because of *it*.

For every story of success, a future marriage that came from being in the right place at the right time, there are examples of the times it failed, whether that was because of circumstances or one's painful decision to move on.

The phrase 'right person, wrong time' may then feel all too applicable for the hostel lifestyle, especially in that moment where one is forced to say goodbye to that certain someone who caught their eye, even if it was only for a few days or perhaps just a single night. It may seem, then, that *keeping* it becomes more difficult than *finding* it.

But what makes dealing with the effects of the double-edged sword a bit easier is that, in a place like this, you never know who is going to walk in that door and change your life, even if you don't know it right away.

7

A bit of the Good, Bad, and Ugly

In conversing with someone from Turkey, China, or Tennessee, that one common thread will often surface—what prompted the decision to come here, now—and from that thought, one may even find shades of themselves in that person they're speaking with. In as many ways as we are different, people are inherently quite similar, and the hostel has a unique way of bringing that out, given the way that complete strangers are thrown together into the same space for several hours or days at a time, forcing each one to step out of their comfort zone and let down their guard for a little while.

As I step back to reflect on it, and how the experience of staying in and working at hostels has changed my life, at times it does feel as if I have become a different person two or three times over in that time, because of the constant change and transiency that is required to keep up with everything as it continues to move. That change, moreover, is as much of what makes the experience worthwhile as it is what makes it so difficult to endure for so long, since the best aspect of it is inherently fleeting, and it can feel like just as you get a hold of it, it is already on its way out the door.

It has become just as clear that, if one embraces a few of the things that the industry stands upon—being open-minded, sociable, and accepting—and applies it to life itself, there is a great deal that can be obtained and experienced, even if it means something that can't be held or touched. The intangible, moreover, is what makes it so difficult at times to write about or articulate to someone who has only heard about hostels but has never set foot in one.

For as much as I had changed while living on the road, I noticed, just as well, a few other backpackers who had chosen this particular way of traveling and living for weeks or months at a stretch, adapting in certain ways to where the environment began to shape them, and how they projected themselves within it.

Occasionally, we'd end up running the circuit and cross paths in different cities, at different hostels that had different dynamics due to their surroundings. At the beach, I would notice how those backpackers embodied a different energy than they did in the city, where the noise and constant stimuli can be as taxing as it is invigorating. In the mountains, or in the desert, their mood might have become more relaxed, inclined to take things slow and easy, and absorb nature in a way they would not be able to do elsewhere. Watching that transformation take place, even if it was ostensibly temporary—and yet, perhaps necessary—in order to experience the place to the fullest, became a fascinating way to study people, and there came even a point where I had to stop to consider how the different environments I moved through might also have been shaping *me*, as I changed scenery and swapped the dirty socks with the clean ones out of that same bag.

Ask those same individuals, and they won't hesitate to tell you about how it can be draining on the psyche, always seeing someone leave or having to explain to the next person who you are, what you're doing, and why you're still here, when they, too, are soon to be on their way out. The toll of being constantly thrust into new social circles, while potentially transformative in its own ways, starts to weigh you down when that's all you know.

It becomes inevitable, at some point, to remonstrate on that lonely thought of 'what if' which lingers when you watch that person you've just built a real connection with pack up their bags and catch the next train out of town, to somewhere else that is new or exotic. The impermanence of it all might make you question what the point is of doing it all over again, even if each day is a new unknown and might procure some profound thought or realization that resonates far beyond the single night you might have spent there.

For all the reasons above, and some others, I considered leaving several times, especially at first. Only to go back *home* to start fresh. But the realization hit me, as I weighed my alternatives, that the road had become *home*. The road that has thrown me countless twists and turns but seems to always bring me back to the thing that makes it so interesting, so compelling, and in fact, quite addictive: the variety, but perhaps even more so, the people.

As evidenced in a place like this, it only takes one person or conversation to spark an idea or inspire a new change of thought toward something, a whole new way of viewing oneself or their circumstances. And yet, at the same time, there's a certain degree of caution that one must exude when conversing with complete strangers, especially if one decides to open themselves up and eventually befriend that stranger, because not every guest that comes through a hostel has the best intentions or bears the same optimistic, open-minded outlook, and before you know it, you might be stuck holding someone else's bag of dirty laundry or old skeletons because you decided to be nice, and lend an ear.

And when it becomes dangerous is when an individual like that recognizes the abundance of intrigue or sincere empathy, and then weaponizes it into something that they can use against the people around them. They say misery loves company, and staying in a place like this long enough will show you just how true that can be for some people, and why the human condition remains so complex and difficult to fully classify.

As rewarding as it can be to be open and embrace each new individual at a hostel, it can be just as imperative not to divulge too much or volunteer unnecessary information right away, especially to the real drifters, the true vagabonds who seem to have just stumbled upon *this place* through some stroke of luck, and want to know what *you're all about*, and whether there's an angle to be had. You might even get to see what *they're* all about, and that there are more of them out there than you might have imagined.

Whether latent or explicit, their eyes can tell you a lot about their intentions. Those eyes might be keen as they carefully sweep the rest of the room, studying your expression to see if it changes when they say certain things. Eventually, they'll have at the ready some story that trumps yours or the other guests in the room, something that will make them seem even more impressive or interesting to that group of curious strangers.

Or sometimes it's in the tone. That sincere interest in the seemingly mundane or the way they casually deflect those questions about themselves, which all but gives them away. The careful threading of a needle that is required to say just enough but not too much about how they got there or how long they plan to stay. The focus, even if feigned, continues to be about *you* and whether you actually have some say in the place or not.

While that answer would depend on the time or place, I knew it was best to deflect the attention, as they were so apt to do, responding instead with questions that could be traced back to a previous answer they gave, trying to catch them ensnared in some simple, but outright, lie, if for no other reason than to affirm that gut feeling that something was off about them from the start, and so that I could excuse myself from the room for no good reason without feeling guilty.

Having seen and conversed with several of these characters, the chameleons and impulsive liars who find their way into hostels all around the world and try to stay as long as possible, the easy deduction is that these individuals are merely lost; perhaps they've been abandoned; perhaps they missed a step somewhere along their path in life and lost course entirely; some are still tumbling; others, fine with the feeling of hitting rock bottom. It is not, one can hope—perhaps naively so—that it was or is their intention to sabotage or usurp the good energy that other travelers or volunteers work so hard to put out and maintain, but rather simply to take what they feel can be given. Even if, in these elements, such a thing, dangerously, can be quite a lot.

The art of knowing how to avoid certain people or situations, then, becomes steadily refined the more time you spend in a place like this. And yet, sometimes they're impossible to avoid, that one person in the kitchen who, as soon as they see you, being that it is so early, and no one else is around, starts asking you questions or to help them solve a problem. Simple conundrums, even, ones that can be solved with a little effort of their own now become yours, and all you wanted was your coffee, a glass of water, or to use the bathroom before going back to bed; and, before you know it, they've occupied so much of your time or stretched your mental bandwidth that you decide, right then and there, that you will do everything you can to avoid them, going forward.

But then—and this has happened to me, more than once—as you part ways, they might leave you with something positive. Perhaps it's a display of gratitude, or even an affirmation of something that you had been ambivalent or curious about, and then you realize that you had more in common than you would have liked to think, while you were eagerly waiting for them to stop talking.

Giving too much of yourself or your time can be a slippery slope, and you can rather quickly find yourself deep in someone else's bag, or perhaps trying to save them, even if it's for just a night. The latter, especially, can mess with your mind and make the heart yearn for something that it knows will be gone soon.

Since it is all so temporary, the space so transient, and the people sometimes so oblivious to it being *shared*, it's best not to get too annoyed or peeved by another person's perceived lack of consideration for sight, sound, or time of day while doing something so simple as mowing down a bag of chips, talking on the phone, or brushing their teeth in the room when the hour is abominably late. Even if they are the ones who can hit the trifecta and complete all three in a single night, it's better to assume they've never stayed in a hostel before and forgive them for their behavior. And if you *do* hold it against them, you might miss out on an opportune connection, a perspective on life, or perhaps even an invitation for a drink later.

8

Mise en Scene: The art of Creating a Good Hostel

How someone experiences a hostel is largely up to them. A dozen people could come to the same hostel on a different—or even the same—day and have a completely different experience than the person in the bunk next to them. One can, just the same, choose to talk to everyone, or absolutely no one.

It became just as clear, as I found myself cycling through hostels, from Chicago to Honolulu, and Portland to South Beach, how the intimacy of a place, and, in turn, the experience itself, can be largely driven by how it is arranged.

A hostel that is too large might inadvertently offer guests too many ways or places to isolate and seclude themselves from other travelers. It is only natural, when we're out of our comfort zone, to fall into the habits we might have built back home, finding an excuse to do something soothing that easily passes the time, but also something that could be done anywhere or at any hour, such as reading a book, practicing guitar, scrolling the phone, or catching up on some trashy reality TV series.

The unfortunate truth about people is that when we have too much space, we tend to find ways to fill it with buffers between us and the outside world, which, in hostels, includes the people, the ones who came there, too, to escape from the monotony of it all and to break their routines for a beat.

And if a hostel is too small, its corridors too tight or common spaces too bleak and sterile to truly feel *comfortable*, guests might hide themselves away in their rooms, only coming out to microwave something for dinner or make some tea, feeling the pressure of forced interaction to be too much, too burdensome on the experience, since they've become so cozy in their cocoons.

That idea of forced interaction, however, is an interesting thing to consider, especially as a proprietor, but also as a guest. Darren Overby—one of the early trailblazers in the US hostel market—first introduced the term 'forced interaction' to me, as we spoke about the intricacies of hostels and how their success can depend greatly upon how they are arranged.

Since his backpacking trip to Europe in 1989, where he was first introduced to hostels, Darren has amassed a great deal of knowledge on the business of hostels and has since become a valuable resource for prospective and current owners with his consulting services. But before getting to the point where other hostel owners would come seeking his opinion, Darren had to learn about the art of hosteling and how much of that can come down to putting people into situations that, although they might not realize it, require them to engage with complete strangers, mostly because they have no other choice.

Darren was like many travelers when he first arrived at a hostel: shy, unsure how to navigate the space, and unsure how his personality would be received by the others. He admitted that at first, he found it difficult to talk to strangers. Then he realized he was only preventing himself from enjoying the experience, so he let it fly.

"I decided that if I wanted to get over it, I would have to try myself on for size. If I put my foot in my mouth, I could always check out," said Darren. So he lent those compliments, flirted when he felt like the moment was right, and told jokes to other guests. The opposite of what Darren expected to happen happened: his energy and presence were well received, not only by his fellow travelers but also by the hostel owners who saw him move so easily within the space, because he was just doing what felt natural.

"I know there's a lot of people like myself (in hostels), who want to say or do something that's natural but don't know how it will be received," said Darren. "But I became this little hub of community by just being myself. Hostels were the vehicle that allowed me to get there."

Seeing that he was becoming an asset to the space, a hostel owner in Europe offered Darren a job. That kick-started his three-decade-long journey into the industry, which entailed Darren owning Pacific TradeWinds Hostel in San Francisco, and also launching Hostelmanagement.com, a database of information on hostels around the globe, which helped establish him as an encyclopedia of knowledge for current and prospective hostel owners in the industry.

That three-plus-decade-long journey into the industry all started because Darren was willing to shed that fear and suspend the uncertainty he felt around being himself, back in that European hostel, when he showed up as a backpacker with a one-way plane ticket and a little over one thousand dollars to his name.

Over the years of traveling through and working at hostels, growing as a person, and gaining valuable insights on the industry that he would later apply as an owner, Darren picked up on a few fundamental things that he saw that separated some hostels from others. Simple things, such as how when a common room overlaps with the reception area, guests tend to interact more, since the ice can be broken over an otherwise transactional or rudimentary experience, such as checking in, resonated with Darren as he cycled through various hostels across Europe.

"The best hostels are designed to have community spaces that are good. Places where it's impossible to avoid interaction with other guests, those are the hostels where it seems like the community flourishes," he explained. That might start at the check-in process, but it can go so far as when someone is brushing their teeth at the sink next to a stranger, or wakes up to see someone stirring awake in the bed opposite them, and has no other choice but to say hello since there are no buffers, no boundaries to hide behind.

Being in those situations might seem uncomfortable at first, but they are fundamental to building the connections and community that so many people seek when booking a hostel in the first place. As a proprietor, breaking down those walls can be as simple as not putting privacy curtains on the bunk beds or making the restrooms a shared space instead of an isolated, single-occupancy room.

"That's where the magic in hostels happens. That's where we feel connected. We have to challenge ourselves with the things that feel risky but are not dangerous," said Darren. "The idea of talking to a stranger feels risky, but it's not dangerous. It's been proven that when humans experience something together that's risky or life-threatening, there's a bonding experience that happens there."

I had also seen this firsthand, how the hostel could be the vessel for bringing out certain things in people they don't expect from themselves.

As I was working on this book, I built a friendship with someone who had no idea he was such a socialite, and would probably tell you he wasn't, but everyone in the room seemed to love him when we would pop into different hostels together. At several different hostels, the guests and staff there picked up on my friend's energy just the same, often embracing him quickly as part of their kin. But when it was just him and me in a different setting, perhaps at his apartment, at the beach, or while grabbing coffee, my friend was much more reserved, less confident in himself, and even questioning many of the trivial things that he made look so easy around other people. He was still the same genuine, likeable person, but only projecting himself differently, based on where he was and who he was around.

Supposing we all do that to some capacity, it's nothing more than a keen observation on how the place can shape the person.

And just the same, the environment—or, the mise en scene, as Darren aptly ascribed it—also gets shaped by the individuals. The vibe of a hostel is ever-changing—it can be altered as soon as a certain person walks through, or out of, that door. Jason, from North Carolina, was a classic example of that. We met in Santa Barbara, where he was stopping through on his way back to Los Angeles before hopping a plane to Europe.

Admittedly, at first, I had one of those, "*this fuckin' guy*" thoughts, when I watched Jason work the common room his first day at the hostel, stopping to talk to nearly every single person about *something*. Frankly, having watched countless others so effortlessly command the energy of the hostel with their intense zeal or loquacious ways, I was reluctant to offer anything more than a 'hello' and easy nod to Jason as we crossed paths in the hallway at first. Perhaps the inclination to not divulge too much about myself, since I had felt the effects of that decision before, had so deeply infected me that I found myself putting up walls when such talkative characters were cycling through the hostel.

But all it took was one overheard conversation in the kitchen between me and another guest to spark a curiosity in Jason, and for him to ask me, as I ate breakfast later that morning, if he could sit down. As an artist himself, my pursuit of some larger, creative work—this very book—had fascinated Jason, and, before I knew it, we were trading suggestions on famous dead authors—throwing praise over certain classics and shaking our fists at others—and, eventually, discussing religion with great ease. In less than an hour, Jason and I had covered a lot of ground, and it felt, as I went to wash my dishes, that I had known him for quite a long time.

This wasn't just a one-off thing, however, and as I spent more time around Jason, sometimes watching him grab the attention of a room full of strangers with his impromptu guitar sessions or by waxing poetic on an ancient scholar or giving the backstory on some iconic song, I saw that it was a large part of his makeup, to be constantly engaging with the people around him, and taking in as much of his environment as he put out.

It came to be quite a regular thing, moreover, to be out with Jason—whether that was in the afternoon on a walk down State Street, or at night, on a busy weekend, when the whole town was out—and to have to wait as he stopped off into a cafe or bar to say hello to someone he had met, or was just jamming with the other day. And what made the whole thing so amusing, yet not surprising, was the fact that Jason had just arrived: *the other day.*

By the time he hit the road again, Jason had essentially become a local and one of those rare guests who felt like they were part of the staff, so it was of little surprise to see and feel how the energy of the place had shifted once he checked out. But travelers like Jason are the ones that you know you'll see again, even if you're not sure where or can't say when, because they share not only that innate curiosity for the world but also the insatiable desire to see as much of it as possible, as long as their circumstances allow. It makes the pursuit of that *thing*, then, feel even more necessary, especially knowing that there are places like this all around the world, the ones that make that realization possible in the first place.

"You can't desire something that you don't even know exists." - Eric Faria.

Being around such seasoned travelers also starts to make international travel seem a lot less intimidating. Since we Americans tend to stick to our usual circuits —a few days in Florida, a quick getaway to see New York City or Chicago, a dusty road trip out West with stops in Las Vegas or the Grand Canyon penciled in— we tend to get comfortable with the idea that there's enough *here* to see to fill a lifetime. While that much might be true, it becomes harder to grapple with that each time you meet someone from another country who has been to four different continents and has a long list of countries still undiscovered.

I'm not saying it's going to be the place you meet your future spouse, or that it will give you the answers you're looking for, but I've seen, heard, and felt the way that it has changed the lives of so many who decided, sometimes on a whim, to try it. There are, I can only presume, thousands of other travelers out there who have found something profound or met someone important while staying in hostels, but all I can speak on is the ones that have told me directly, and echoed the sentiment that I have often expressed: that the hostel experience—although unrealized at the time —changed my life, and shaped who I was.

It comes as little surprise, then, as to why some people decide to spend several months, or even years, living in that constant cycle of newness, because, if one is so willing, there is always something to be learned, whether that is about oneself or the world around them.

9

Pourquoi? - The Beauty of Language

I t can be a funny feeling, being the only American in the room, trying to keep up with each traveler and what they're saying about here, there, us, them, soaking in that cross stitch of cultures which occurs so seamlessly, even if the accents are sometimes so thick that all you can do is nod and pretend that you are following along. For as much as they might try to appease you with English, it can be hard for a foreigner *not* to slip back into their native tongue, especially when there might be others in the room who speak it. The excitement is sometimes hard to contain when they find out at least one other person can understand how they're thinking, and so now they don't have to be so diplomatic or surface-level with certain matters.

As stimulating as it can be, to sit in a room with new acquaintances and listen to them rattle off a multitude of different languages, it also becomes conflicting, as one starts to notice that so many Americans rely entirely on English; at best, unless it is something they were brought up with, a lot of Americans might only know a little bit of Spanish, or perhaps a few phrases in French, German, or Portuguese, whereas many of the international travelers who come *here* are fluent in two, three, sometimes four, different languages. While much of that has to do with the culture and how English is emphasized from an early age in other countries, it's hard not to feel like one is immediately behind the ball when it comes to breaking bread with those foreigners or accessing different parts of the world through language.

And yet as much as language is a tool to get around and navigate places or people, it's also a sign of respect; learning even fragments of a foreign language can open doors that were otherwise unimaginable or unreachable, and it often only requires a bit of practice and willingness to learn. And like a muscle, that exercise of using another language needs to be refined, and practiced at least occasionally, and even if that 'muscle' has no other purpose but to be shown off in those rooms, knowing how and when to use it can be quite valuable, especially given how eclectic the hostel and its occupants can be on any given day.

Swapping slang words tends to be a good place to start. Whether that's calling them 'trousers' instead of pants, quantifying an item in 'heaps', or ascribing something cool as 'class', I've learned a thing or two by being inquisitive with international travelers in hostels, and those same foreigners are often just as fascinated by the way we Americans use terms like 'bet', 'low key', or 'drip'.

I often think back to a certain St. Patrick's Day that I spent at a hostel in San Diego, when I found myself listening to a pair of 20-something backpackers on the patio banter back and forth about the day, and what they were going to do about it.

The two happened to be from Ireland, and once I made mention of the holiday, they were insistent, saying, "Mate. It's *not* like this over in Ireland. Americans celebrate St. Patrick's Day more than we do."

This was hardly the first time I had heard the Irish chortle about how the Americans had hijacked their holiday, using it as yet another excuse to be drinking from breakfast until the lights came on at last call. As I listened to the two Irish mates banter and bust one another's chops, I couldn't help but shake my head and laugh, astonished at their breadth of slang, wishing, in that moment, that I had a notebook at the ready, instead of a joint.

As the joint got passed around, we talked about more of the cultural differences between our two countries, and it wasn't long before that word "football" came up, and I had to defend, for the umpteenth time, Americans stealing that, too.

It so happened that one of the guys had quite an extensive knowledge of American football, and the conversation quickly turned into the two of us discussing his agonizing affection for Cleveland's team, the dramatic saga of Aaron Rodgers, and what was to come in the next month's draft, all while his mate stood there looking at us, incredulous but increasingly bored, as if *we* were speaking another language.

I spent many nights on that same patio with Vince and Camilla, who would sometimes invite a few of their Italian friends in the city to come through the hostel, usually to smoke a whole pack of cigarettes or put down a few bottles of wine on the patio while they chopped it up.

As one who did not know the language, but was regularly invited into those circles, I found it curious—but also inspiring—being around a foreign tongue that was going off like rapid fire, that I could loosely understand at least *some* of what they were saying. It's no secret that Italians will use their hands to get certain points across; nonverbal gestures are as integral to the language as the words themselves. That much I had learned as a child, and from spending a bit of time there several years prior. So even though I was not entirely clear about *what* my Italian friends were talking about, I found myself able to catch certain things, seeing *how* they said it, and, based on the subsequent reaction, what it meant to the ones listening.

The beauty of hostels is that there is usually a whole mix of languages going around, but the flipside of that is that, while you might hear certain things that you want or even need to hear, there will be some things that you do not. Whether that's someone giving a detailed account of their cycle, or how they decided to use a shower mat as their towel since they had so carelessly forgotten to grab one before getting into the tub, I can assure you: some things are better left unheard.

Day or night, the value of having earplugs or a solid pair of headphones cannot be overstated—a way to block out noise, not only, but also a symbol of being somewhere else, even when you're in the same room as someone who is almost *too* affable and always has something to say—because, there will usually always be someone around who wants to talk.

Even if they have nothing planned for the day, that doesn't mean you don't. And there's no nice way to explain it other than to find somewhere else to be; if that's not an option, the next best thing is to plug in the headphones and pretend to be completely focused on something else—anything—so that they get the message that you're not trying to talk. At least not at the moment, but perhaps later, after some of the work has been done or enough coffee has been consumed.

10

Becoming Comfortable
With
the Uncomfortable

"If you asked hostel guests what they wanted out of a hostel, I don't know if they would tell you what they really want," said Darren Overby. "What they'll tell you is typically the physical attributes. A self-service kitchen, privacy curtains on the beds. But privacy is the exact opposite of what builds community."

Many travelers choose hostels as a way to save money. While this is true—they are cheaper than the average hotel—there are certain benefits of hosteling that transcend saving a few dollars, such as the feeling of being *a part* of something. Connections can happen just about anywhere in a hostel, at any time, but they can just as easily be avoided, if one is not comfortable yet with the feeling of being uncomfortable; understanding as much, Darren, in his nearly three decades as a hostel owner in San Francisco, was adamant about arranging the space into somewhere where people had no choice *but* to interact with one another.

"If everyone is cocooned in their space, they don't connect as much," said Darren. "When you happen to be in your bed and you wake up and see someone across from you, it can be awkward. But you introduce yourself, and then now it's a little less awkward, because now we know each other's names."

Of course, it's a bit weird at first, sleeping above or sharing bathrooms with someone of the opposite sex, especially if you are accustomed to certain privacies or personal amenities while traveling. But sooner or later, you have to swallow your pride and not overthink it when you find yourself using the bathroom in the stall next to that attractive backpacker who might have smiled at you over breakfast, or when you have to shave or put on deodorant while a complete stranger is fixing their makeup or brushing their teeth in the sink next to you.

Being uncomfortable with the uncomfortable is, after all, necessary to unlocking all that the hostel experience has to offer, and that might even entail trying to erase from memory the sight of someone older guest, who knows better, but still walks bare-assed through the bathroom and smiles at you, without a care in the world, on their way to the shower.

The constant activity, the demand of being *always available*, the seemingly endless cycle of new conversations that follow similar lines, can become quite the double-edged sword.

On one hand, that constantly revolving pool of people from all over the planet, who come trotting through for a few days at a time, may become an unexpected catalyst for future travel plans to a place that wasn't even on the radar until you met that person. Even if you, personally, are not the one offering the physical accommodations, there will be those who promise to return the favor and put *you* up when you come to *their* country.

Realizing this, rather early on, was partly what compelled me to stay as long as I had, which, at times, felt like a few months too long—but in that same time, I learned how necessary it is to sometimes just say no. Perhaps just as crucial as knowing how and when to say no is knowing how to hide—particularly as a volunteer—or at least disguise oneself so that some degree of separation is provided between the workplace and the personal life, since they so suddenly become one and the same.

From his early days of running hostels, Gayle Burgundy would talk about how several of his staff at the infamous Zoo Hostel in San Diego decided to start wearing wigs while making their way out of the hostel, so as not to be stopped by a guest over something trivial or a problem that could be solved by the person *actually* on shift. So when Gayle saw Kai, one of his managers at the time, slip out of her bedroom window after her shift at the hostel, just so as not to have to walk through the lobby, since she was sure to be stopped for *something*, he fell into a fit of laughter.

"I've done that one before!" roared Gayle, adding that he wasn't upset with Kai. In fact, he was proud of her.

It takes being crafty sometimes just to establish *some* level of normalcy toward a job that is in many ways rather unconventional, as it requires one to be both physically and emotionally present even when they do not necessarily want to be, since *they* live there, too. Finding things outside of the workplace, then, is one way to build separation from the work that seems to never end, and that can be as simple as finding recreational activities or classes in town, or simply establishing the habit of being *off-site* as soon as the shift is up. Disguise or no disguise.

Kai, having done the volunteer program in several countries around the world, knows as well as anyone that there are secrets to keeping the job fresh, finding ways to not get burned out by the constant recycling of energy that is required to make the experience interesting and fun for the next guest who checks in.

For as nice as it is to be regularly invited somewhere, and to constantly have new and often interesting people around, always taking in their energies and hearing funny stories or fresh perspectives, it becomes essential to establish boundaries, if not for anyone but yourself. The result of *not* doing that may lead to one burning a bridge they might have just spent months building, or souring otherwise healthy relationships without meaning to, simply from the fatigue of constantly being *available*.

Watching it burn people out in real time, as I have, is certainly disappointing, since there *does* seem to be a way to have both. For as invigorating and even intoxicating as the bohemian vibe and open-armed approach of a hostel can be, there *is* such a thing as overstaying a welcome, and that goes for both the staff and the ones who are merely stopping through. It becomes just as easy to forget that the experience is meant to be temporary, no matter how easy it is to assimilate oneself into the lifestyle.

11

A few of the Trade-offs

D o this long enough and you're bound to hit a wall, or at least endure a few more sleepless nights than you hoped for—unless you're so flush with cash that you can book out private rooms for long enough to create some actual separation from you and the rest of the people. While the people are usually well-intended, sometimes it's the little things, the ones they can't help, like the snoring that wakes you from a deep sleep and leaves you wondering, *Why me?*

That was the story of me and Sammy, the guest who somehow always ended up booking the same room as I had on his random, but frequent stops in San Diego one summer. Sammy would pop into San Diego for a few days to work, and then be gone, so the hostel staff gave him leniency on the 14-day policy, since he always paid up and was never a problem. The problem was, whenever Sammy showed up, he inexplicably always chose the bed above mine—even when there might have been several empty bunks in the room.

Sammy arrived late one night, as he usually did, somewhere past midnight, waking me only briefly when he climbed the ladder to his bed, the metal frame of the bunk rocking as Sammy made his way up the ladder. After listening to him wrestle for a moment and then finally fall asleep, I did the same.

Sometime later, I was jolted awake. It was Sammy, his snoring sounding like a symphony that had just started. Without even having to check the time, I knew that it was four a.m., give or take fifteen minutes on either end. I knew this because that was about the time when Sammy would hit his deep REM cycle, and he was as heavy a snorer as I had ever been around, often waking several others in the room. As it had that night, it became like clockwork, watching the distant glow from each of the phones from other guests in their beds flickering on as they, too, felt the moment of pain, realizing that Sammy's snoring was probably not going to stop anytime soon.

That night, there was a girl, perched above and across from me in an opposite bunk bed. She flew up out of bed angrily, looking first down at me, and then over at Sammy. We caught eyes for a moment, and then she whispered to me, "Kick the bed."

"I'm sorry?" I laughed.

The girl clicked her tongue and then hissed, "*Kick* the bed."

But I couldn't do that to old Sammy, my insufferable bunkmate for the foreseeable future; I shook my head and chuckled, enraging the girl even further. Finally, seeing that I was not going to be an accomplice, the girl glowered at me before grabbing something off her bed and throwing it at Sammy.

Sammy's violent snoring suddenly stopped. He jostled in his bed for a second before falling asleep again. The lights on each phone in the room gradually extinguished, and everyone went back to sleep.

While most hostel guests are polite, friendly, and otherwise respectful of the space, during high seasons, especially, it can feel like a game of roulette, where you don't quite know what you'll get on any given night since the place is full. There can be someone like Sammy with whom you're stuck in the same room for the next four days, since the place is full. There can be a guest that stinks, but no one in the room is courageous enough to single them out to the staff, so the rest of the room suffers from the aroma of old socks, bad body odor, or something they ate earlier that night. There might even be that one guest who brings another person into their bed in the dead of night, thinking no one else will know the better, but it's quite obvious what is going on, and there's no easy way of trying to interrupt *that*.

However, if someone is being truly insufferable or flat-out rude, it usually isn't too long before someone else in the room yanks their privacy curtain aside and says something, or at least gives a vile glare. It's amazing, just the same, how many people still need to be told.

Whether they're not accustomed to sharing space, or they simply don't care, that's part of the double-edged sword of always having someone new around. For as beautiful and full of optimism as they might be, they can be quite ugly, too.

As staff, but also as a guest, that revolving door of people can also make one start to question someone's intentions when they do something nice or unexpected, even if it does seem like it is out of the kindness of their hearts, because it only takes once for someone to randomly gift you something that is worth a considerable sum: a bottle of booze, a bag of weed, or even a pair of shoes that they haven't worn since they bought: no strings attached.

But then, sometime later, perhaps when that person finds themselves in a situation, needing a favor, or expecting you to bend a rule for them, to do something you're not comfortable with, they might say, "Remember that time I gave you..."

It might even just so happen that someone has become a different person since you first met them. You might check someone in at the start of the week, or have breakfast together, reading them as being a certain way or even befriending them, perhaps sharing a night out together, and by the time Saturday rolls around, they've let it all hang out, and may even have embarrassed themselves by getting a bit too carried away, and now suddenly they are not in the loop about the next social gathering or are subtly ousted by the others.

And so what you see is not always what you get, and having the constant exposure to a myriad of people and personalities, sometimes all at once, can easily exemplify that.

The litany of personalities, the things people are willing to do or have even done to get there, is part of what makes the whole setup so fascinating and, in its own way, quite addictive—that temporary holdover of a home steadily eases you in and becomes more comfortable the more you see others do the same.

"So, you all just *live* here?" a guest might ask, once they notice you've been around for a while or watched you exit a room that says 'staff only'. And then the questions start coming in. "How many of you are there? What are the hours like? *Oh*...Are there any openings?"

You might, later that day, encounter one of the folks who take up most of your energy—sometimes there's more than one of them in the house at once. It can feel as if you are tasked, then, with suddenly managing what feels like a mix of misbehaving children or insecure teenagers who are gossiping, even complaining about something they saw someone do or say in the other room, and you have to be the one to find ways to separate them.

One of them might even stop and tell you about something that happened before you've clocked in, or even put the coffee on, before anyone else is awake and wants you to do something about it—since you live here, too, they remind you.

Filtering truths, then, and finding ways to pick up on pantomimes to catch someone in a harmless lie or perhaps just a tiny exaggeration, becomes a useful skill, one that can even become refined in a place like this, since that exposure to all types of people is as broad as it is consistent. And yet still, people will always be people.

They may even become territorial, taking up sometimes large amounts of the space that is supposed to be for someone else. Or they may complain, and want *you* to solve one of their obscure problems or resolve even the smallest issues—such as their room being too cold because another guest left the window open, perhaps one of their bunkmates was farting all night, or maybe there was more rain than they expected when they booked their trip—or even the bigger ones, like trying to have someone else thrown out for allegedly doing *something*; if you're not careful, that might just become a game of 'he said, she said'.

At some point, you need to take *someone's* word, because it is your job to keep the peace and make sure the place is running smoothly, even if that means trying to simply stop someone from trying to police other guests on the house rules.

While these characters do exist, the ones who do actively set out to ruffle the feathers, or even see how many feet they can take after having been given an inch of leeway, their presence is however, far outweighed by the kind, ambitious American or open-minded backpacker who shares stories about their wild escapades overseas, or invites you on a day trip with them to some nearby town.

If it is not yet evident, hostels can provide you with a little bit of everything—or even a lot of something—all at once. You might meet the most charismatic person you've ever met, but even if they appear to be harmless and well-intentioned, all it takes is one episode for the entire situation to unravel. One night out, and all of their demons are exposed to the world. A little too much to drink and they suddenly become a liability not only to themselves but also to the rest of the party, ready to punch, or be punched, on the short walk back from the town square. Without intending to, they may provide insight into why they are where they are and why they constantly request extensions, even after the 14-day period ended.

For as many things as they are, hostels are still also a *business*, and by letting one person bend the rules or take certain liberties, you can open the door to something much bigger, where suddenly the bottom dollar doesn't matter. Losing out on a sale might be tough to stomach, but keeping the ship upright and the vibe steady is perhaps most consequential for an operation like this to run as it is designed, since it becomes something that is much bigger than the individual by relying so heavily upon the individuals: a true sum of all its parts.

And yet, the folks who are out of pocket, a little unhinged, and speak, perhaps a bit too often, without a filter, are a large part of what makes this whole social experiment so compelling and illustrative of human nature. Even if conversing with a particular individual takes patience and putting the judgments aside as to *how* they've become that way and what baggage or past trauma they might be hanging onto, it's important to remember that they deserve an opportunity to share the experience, too.

The experience may, just as well, however, become the most comfortable or stress free thing someone has had or experienced in some time, so it can be heartbreaking, watching someone old enough to be your mother, who seems to have just found that *thing* they were looking for—a place where they can fly under the radar and not have to worry about using their social security check or life savings on rent — be told that it is time to leave because they've reached the end of their 14 days. Naturally, they grow upset and may even cause a scene, unable to understand when the person behind the desk says: It's just policy.

Bending the rules just once or with a certain thing becomes a slippery slope, and suddenly it's that much easier to be lax toward the next guest, who has found themselves in that same boat. The point of a hostel, however, is to be a placeholder, not a permanent place of residency. To ensure that, most hostels in the States generally enforce a strict 14-day policy, which prohibits a guest from staying for more than two weeks within a calendar year. Such a thing exists to prevent someone from getting too comfortable, and just because their money is green, too, doesn't mean that having them around the hostel for months at a time is necessarily good for business.

So while it can be hard watching that sad, old traveler, who felt like they had just figured out how to make it work, break down and cry in front of a whole room of strangers, and plead for just a little bit of compassion from that person behind the desk, who is trying to keep it together and not cave, it's important to remember that this might simply be the situation that that person has found themselves in, and there is only so much that a place like this can do to help them along the way.

113

12

When too Much of a Good Thing Becomes bad

I n theory, the idea of bringing together people from all walks of life and putting them into a single space is profound and part of what makes the hostel experience so special and unique to travel. But in practice, that concept can pose some hurdles, especially for hostel owners and staff, because, as bountiful as the beautiful souls and ambitious, wide-eyed travelers who traverse them are, one might just as well cross paths with a bad apple or deceitful individual.

The larger the scale of the business, the more opportunities these characters have to linger and slowly settle in, especially once they've identified an access point or point of vulnerability within the staff that can be exploited. And especially as that operation grows in scale, the owners will not always be on-site, protecting the thing they built, overseeing the garden.

Nor will they be able to suddenly clean house as might be necessary, in the case that the rot is coming from within.

Bad seeds come in all shapes and sizes. Whether it's an individual inside the operation, actively trying to bring it down, or some guy on the couch who has been through it all and will unabashedly tell you about it. And so that bohemian, all-friendly environment of a hostel can become a perfect place for such pathological liars or highly trained con-artists to dig in and sell a whole bag of lies to whoever is willing to listen. That revolving door of faces creates an endless supply of 'fresh bait' for these individuals to embellish their life stories, exaggerate their accomplishments, or amplify their miseries. Since most hostel guests are simply looking for a good time and are happy to listen to each new story, those lies can live on, even if it is as simple as what that person has done, where they came from, or where they are going.

Perhaps harmless on the surface, these lies or mild acts of deceit can be a detriment to the place of business, because someone can quickly get the wrong idea about not only the operation, but also the ones who own it. I had been on my way through a hostel in Southern California when I witnessed something like this play out.

As I stood at the front desk of the hostel, chatting with Gayle Burgundy, who had just come in to pull a shift, a woman approached us and quickly asked Gayle if he was the owner of this business. Gayle smiled and warmly introduced himself as, indeed, the owner. The woman nodded and then dashed off to the patio, where there was another guest, a man, lying out in one of the chairs, bathing in the sun, nursing a beer; it was hardly eleven o'clock. From the reception desk, we could hear the woman's voice rise and shake with anger, accusing the fellow of proclaiming to be someone he was not. Their argument grew heated, and finally she walked off. Gayle could only shake his head and laugh, explaining to me that this was not the first time he had seen such a thing happen.

The man outside, who we later learned to have been posing as the owner of the hostel for the length of his stay, checked out within the next few days, and in the meantime, did just about everything he could to avoid any interaction with Gayle, the *real* owner. Things at the hostel resumed as normal, but that small incident illustrated how pervious a place like this can be, especially when there is someone with a lie to spread and the people with real skin in the place are not on-site, or even aware of what is going on.

Strangely enough, a similar scenario played out again a few months later, when I was at a different hostel in Los Angeles.

It was early fall, and I was sitting in the lounge, watching a football game on my laptop, when a guy my age sat down at the wide table next to me. We got to chatting, and it wasn't long before he asked me who I was, what I was all about, and where I was going next. I took my eyes off the game and began explaining a bit about this book and how I had started traveling in hostels in the first place. He was somewhat in awe and wanted to know more about the hostel we were both staying at and how it started.

"Oh, isn't this place owned by a couple of young women?" the guy asked.

"No, actually. A couple of guys founded it a while back, in San Diego."

Not unlike the woman who asked about who owned the hostel in Santa Barbara, the guy's expression changed quite suddenly. His eyes narrowed as he looked at me.

"No, it was started by a couple of women," he contested. "*They* own this place."

I hesitated, knowing that what *I* said was true, and that while the guy could have easily been misinformed, perhaps he had some angle behind what *he* was saying to be true.

"Actually, they don't," I said, holding back my laughter. "I can tell you for a fact that it's owned by a couple of guys. I know them personally."

"Uh huh...And what did you say your name was?" The guy looked at me, tilting his head as he spoke in a tenor that seemed almost threatening, as if to suggest that he was filing away the information for a later time, for when he would report me to the *real owners*. I let out a chortle and then gave him my name, first and last.

"Right," the guy said, a bit of skepticism still lingering in his voice. "Well, I'm going to make some food. It was nice to meet you, Zack…"

I sat there, replaying the conversation in my head, trying to make sense of what had just happened and how *this* was the type of thing I had been warned about by Gayle and other hostel owners who had to learn how to manage the duality of their own success.

I was hardly shocked, then, to hear the same guy from the lounge arguing in the kitchen with the manager, who was a soft-spoken, gentle girl from Ecuador. She and I had become friends during my time staying there, and not once did I hear her lose her cool or even raise her voice.

"Sir, you need to wash your dishes," the manager was saying firmly. "You cannot leave them in the sink like that. Please clean up after yourself so others do not have to."

"I did!" the guy cried out. "Look. I washed my dishes! Why are you giving me problems, lady? You're crazy!"

"No, sir. You did *not*. You walked away from your mess in the sink. I watched you do it," replied the manager, her voice slightly shaking.

"Damn, lady, leave me alone! I washed my dishes! Why are you calling me out?"

From where I sat, I could not see the two of them in the kitchen, but knew that the manager was starting to lose patience, the way her tone continued to become more direct.

"Sir, I can pull up the cameras and show you. It is not our responsibility as staff to clean up after our guests. Everyone is supposed to do their own dishes; it is house rules. There is even a sign that says so. If you do not cooperate, I am sorry, but I will have to ask you to leave, because you are not following house rules."

The guy continued to contest his case but eventually gave up and was escorted down the hall to get his stuff out of his room. On his way out, he began insulting the manager, saying how he was going to complain to the owners about how he was just mistreated by the staff.

"Please, go ahead," said the manager, fuming as she showed him the door.

I sat there, staring at my computer, only able to shake my head and laugh, thinking about characters like him and the way they can so quickly flip a switch and become someone else.

As much as they can be an incubator for growth and change, hostels can also be an escape for some people. They might see the volunteer program as a solution, others might view the hostel as a perfect place to party for a few weeks at a throw, and then move on. But, as Bobby Dyer said to me, at some point, the party will end, and people need to go home.

While hostels may offer a range of enriching and memorable experiences, they can, just as well, allow one to shirk growing up, providing a way around some of the hard constructs in life for a while. With utilities and the mortgage taken care of, and new people to share stories, a six-pack, or a meal out with, the idea of setting up shop can sound quite compelling.

Things are good here, so why *would* I leave?

I have been guilty of it myself, but also seen others say, with firm conviction, that they will be heading out next month, and not to worry about putting them on the schedule. Until the end of the month rolls around and the idea of staying far outweighs the alternative, which is a return to some degree of reality.

Especially in a place like this, some people talk the talk, and others walk the walk. Seeing that play out enough in real time, I started to condition myself to believe about 70% of what someone was saying, at least when I first met them—though that figure seems generous, now. Applying certain filters is imperative while traveling, because on the road, it's easy to be impressionable, especially in a place like this, where there is such a high degree of activity, and much of the experience itself is driven by how open and accepting one decides to be to the buffet of interesting people and conversation. But where that becomes dangerous is when you start to believe nearly everything that is being said around you, by other travelers or even the ones in charge of curating the experience, be that the story about that night that person spent in jail, or the amazing house they have somewhere in the hills, that celebrity they know, the great job they have back home.

It's easy to think that these white lies are nothing more than surface-level exaggerations to make the conversation easy, or to make a person seem more interesting than they might be. But with enough traction, from even the smallest embellishment, that person can create a whole new story, of someone who has lived one of the most unusual or harrowing of lives, and suddenly *that* is how they are perceived, instead of as the person they actually are, when they are not also around a room full of strangers who will almost certainly be gone in a few days.

Deciding how and when to apply that gradient of discerning someone's intentions is an artful balance, especially for those who commit to the lifestyle for stretches at a time. Kai Sills, who spent years doing the volunteer program in other countries before becoming a manager of a hostel in Santa Barbara, acknowledged in one of our conversations the especially unique dynamic of building trust and relationships in such a transient place.

"As a guest, the experience is much different, because when you're traveling, everything is always new," Kai said to me one day. "So you're a lot more willing to take something as it is, or believe what someone says. But when you know that person for an extended period of time, you might not be as willing to believe them."

Being lenient with certain guests and ignoring the 14-day policy, as some hostel staff might decide to do, can make it feel like there are phases that occur in the hostel, with specific characters embedding themselves so deeply in the fiber of the place that it begins to reflect them in many ways. It can go both ways, with that person being like a light, a warm fixture to the place, or a sound figure that becomes as integral to the flow and vibe of the place as the staff themselves. And then, before you know it, you start to know one another's tendencies, schedules, or preferences to such a high degree that it is hard *not* to feel like they're family, sharing the same house but also depending on its sanctity.

Sometimes, however, that individual wears out their welcome and is one day asked to leave, all while wondering even how it got to that point. Only once that person moves on does that era or phase within the constant cycle of change become realized, whether that was mostly positive or quite toxic.

Perhaps just as fascinating is that, if you spend enough time on the circuit, you'll start to see the same faces. Still partying. Still on the hunt for that apartment. Still talking up that creative project or hoping to land that great job they've been talking about for weeks.

Sometimes that's in a different city, or even a different state, you might see them at a different hostel, months or even years later, leaving you to wonder how they've managed to talk their way into staying beyond the 14 day policy, or if they've traded out a few months of their time to do the volunteer program somewhere so as to float and stack some cash before moving on again.

The latter is one way to thread the needle, but it can be difficult to cycle to break, given how comfortable the place can be and how ever-changing it can seem. Given that the lifestyle is one way of always having something new at your fingertips and someone to share it with, it can, just as well, quickly set its grips into someone and sink deeper and deeper with every day or week that passes. Because here, the future is just a concept, as there's always something going on today—so why stress about work or finding other arrangements?

13

The Little Things That Mean a lot

O ne of the best parts about being an American, staying in American hostels, is having the opportunity to show foreigners *our* holidays. Celebrating the USA in style: letting it all hang out for Mardi Gras, putting on excessive spreads for Thanksgiving, or shooting off a whole village's worth of fireworks on the 4th of July. Watching the excited foreigners get all decked out in festive gear, being over glutinous, or binge drinking because that's just what you do here, is worth the price you might all pay the next day.

Being in any one spot for long enough can even make you feel like a local, and so when that foreign traveler—or perhaps another American who had not ventured that far in this direction yet—shows up and says they're interested in seeing the sights around town, or take part in an activity that can only be done *here*, you get to play guide, acting like someone who has lived there for much of your life, when really this is just another dot on the map.

Whereas the idea might have been only to travel there, suddenly, you might find yourself smitten with the idea of establishing roots there, and actually becoming a resident, at least for a while, since there now seems to be an easy way to do that.

It is because of that realization, I suppose, that some do what they can to stick around such idyllic spots and eventually land apartments, find lovers, or secure good jobs so that it is *not* just a blip on the radar for them.

The wide range of different languages, cuisines, and cultural differences that one is exposed to while staying at a hostel is part of what makes the experience so unique and especially transformative, but, just as fascinating is the wide range of economic brackets that one might encounter in the same room at any given moment, and how that, too, might also show us that we are a lot more alike than we are different.

Being that many hostel guests are on tight budgets —some will even laugh about how they can barely afford the beer they're drinking—accepting the charity of another traveler might feel strange. But as you get to know that generous stranger, you might realize that *this* is what they were looking for—perhaps they weren't even looking for it, but rather stumbled upon it because they decided to try something new and step out of their comfort zone for a few days at a time.

Larry was someone who had never been to a hostel before but had decided to book one since it was half the price of that cozy seaside hotel down the street that he often frequented while in Santa Barbara for work. When he pulled up, a few others and I at the hostel had just been gathering people to go out for a trip to a local taqueria. Larry set his bags down, threw on a clean shirt, and came along for the walk. He was like countless other travelers who had come through the hostel, a bit quiet at first but interested in the concept and even amazed at the little things like the free breakfast, daily activities, and the number of travelers his age.

Larry and I chatted a bit on the way to the taqueria, but it wasn't until the next morning that I saw him, after breakfast, writing in his planner. I asked him what he was up to that day, since I had some work to do myself but wanted to take advantage of the nice weather and perhaps go to the beach in Isla Vista. Immediately, Larry volunteered to drive us over there once he finished up his work. We met up a few hours later in the parking lot and got into his decked-out BMW. As we got to talking, Larry told me about what he did, why he was in Santa Barbara, and his life growing up. Unabashedly, he shared stories about some of the hardships he had, running with the wrong crowd, and almost going down the wrong path. He had lived a life that was tougher than most people I had known, and endured enough tribulations that could have made for a Hollywood script. There was, however, no 'woe is me' spin on Larry's outlook toward life, only a determination to not only appreciate the small and beautiful things it brought, but also to share them with others. So when it came time to pay for our goods at the weed shop, and before that, a few enormous breakfast burritos from the hole-in-the-wall spot that Larry knew of along the way, he insisted on paying for everything.

"Pay it forward," said Larry, batting my hand away each time I pulled out my wallet. "I've been blessed to be where I am now. I have a good job. I'm fortunate enough not to have to worry about money right now, so don't worry about it. Pick up the tab for the next guy."

With our sack lunches and bag of weed, we walked the bluffs in Isla Vista and chatted more about life, and some of the small realizations that make it easier to navigate, such as working hard and treating others how you wanted to be treated. What stuck out to me, other than Larry's generosity, was how I had just recently befriended another fellow who was nearly twice Larry's age and had endured similar adversities and struggles in life, but had found a similarly higher way of living, which was nothing more than spreading goodwill through small acts of charity and positive affirmations. Many of the things Larry said on our walk that day were echoed by my older friend, and I often found myself finishing Larry's sentences.

While brief, encounters like the one I had with Larry only reaffirmed how easily the hostel can bring certain people into your life, and beyond just the natural beauty of the places you might explore together, it is so often the things that are said or actions that leave lasting, if not profound, impressions and new ways of looking at the world.

It happens in hostels all around the world, ostensibly every day, two strangers who suddenly become friends, and then they're spending all of their time together, as if *that* is the sort of thing they needed when they booked a bed for the night. That connection becoming a way to take the mind off the frustrations of life, a reason to not have to think about the opposite sex for a while, or perhaps someone to talk about some of the deeper things in life with, and then, if lucky, that stranger becomes a pal to plan a future trip with, since that travel lust or an insatiable curiosity for the world is something both people share.

A single connection between two guests might then even begin to swallow up several others, and suddenly there's a whole squad of you, spending your days lounging at the beach, booking cars together to see some of the area's top-rated sights, or tearing it up at a few of the local dive bars in town and not leaving until last call.

It is not a stretch, then, to say that the opportunity to encounter like-minded people is one of the main reasons so many travelers decide to continue staying at hostels. And for those who are not fully aware of their benefits, perhaps since they have not stayed at one — or, simply, the right one — it usually comes eventually, and so then it is no surprise when they stroll up to the reception desk and ask about extending for another night — perhaps, two, if there is still availability.

It's not always the late nights out or impromptu day trips out of town together that can come from merely saying 'hello' to someone you don't know— sometimes it is as simple and satisfying as sharing the one thing that keeps us all alive.

Meg Dismer, who started out with ITH Hostels back when the company first began, spoke on the beauty of sharing meals in hostels, and how that lone ritual can so effortlessly become the connective tissue that brings people together in such a fluid and transient space. Having come up in a hostel culture where communal dinners and pancake breakfasts were an integral part of the guest experience, Meg saw firsthand how simply sharing a meal from one's childhood or home country could transform someone's stay and turn it into a travel experience that is quite unlike any other.

"Sharing food creates this environment where everyone belongs and conversation is expected," said Meg. "It creates a space where people can naturally connect in the most fundamentally human way."

For guests, getting a free breakfast or being treated to a taste of someone's old family recipe can be a pleasant surprise—an unexpected perk of the experience—but as staff, that shared responsibility of preparing food for one another every night can become the thing that strengthens the bond within a team, and, whether that's cutting down onions for a sauce, or sticking around after dinner to help dry and put away dishes, that bond can also be what helps keep those teams together.

Gayle Burgundy, a seasoned hostel vet, once said to me, "A staff that eats together, stays together."

And, having spent months bouncing between several hostels, falling in with different teams of volunteers for various lengths of time, I saw firsthand just how true that could be. Some of the best meals, moreover, that I have eaten over the last several years came from some foreign traveler inside of a hostel who knew their mother's recipe like the back of their hand and were simply glad to share it with others.

I witnessed, just as well, how, at one hostel, the volunteers might all put tremendous amounts of effort into their required task of cooking staff meals every night, taking pride in their opportunity to show off their cultural heritage through a few of their favorite recipes, while at other locations, some merely skated by, dumping a can of chili beans into a pot and calling it dinner. It came as little surprise, then, to see how the chemistry within those two different teams varied, and how that even was felt from the guests, since so much of the culture starts from the top down, and how, moreover, so much of that culture can be created by simply taking the time to sit around the table together and chat over a hot meal.

14

The Things we Need to Hear Sometimes

"There's never really a *good* time to go. You'll always find some reason *not* to, something that will make you think about it until you overthink it, and end up not going, after all. So what I've learned," said Vincent, the German backpacker I met in San Diego, who was preparing to head south, first through Central America, and then eventually to Brazil, "is that you just need to get on that bus. Once you're on the train, the bus, the airplane that's taking you to where you want to go, everything melts away. The hard part is over. But you have to first get yourself there. Once you do, you don't look back."

For one who developed somewhat early in life an itch for travel, it wasn't long before I started staying in hostels that I noticed how they tend to attract that same type of spirit—someone who is as invigorated by the unknown or as stirred by the slightly uncomfortable as much as they are by the beautiful sights, the open road, and the interesting people—and how, although the hostel may open doors to all the above, they are often gateways to the things we need to hear, like the advice from Vincent, to *just go*.

In the same way, working at a hostel, watching them pack up their bags, strapping that extra pair of shoes to the back, or stuffing that water bottle in whatever pocket it can fit, and then *just going* can, just the same, foment a strange feeling of envy. It might feel even if you are stuck living out someone else's dream, since there will always be a new adventure to hear about, some grand expedition that is on the horizon and how it will finally check off a few of those bucket list items of lore, but you have to stay put, and clean up after that rowdy group of backpackers or that insightful nomad once they've hit the road, and then live vicariously through their beautiful photographs or the occasional text messages.

That can be a strange feeling indeed, and remonstrating on it may either inspire you to find ways to get back into the wild, where the road may be invigorating as it is, at times, challenging; or, it may send you down a deep well of regrets that will leave you wondering why you chose to try to cling onto something that is inherently so fleeting.

Ryan was in the middle of recounting all of the places he lived after having spent the first part of his life growing up in Canada—the accent, impossible to

disguise; the warm disposition, just as inconcealable —
when he stopped to ask, "Would you like to smoke?"

Remembering I was on a streak of abstinence, I
took a moment to consider his offer before saying yes.

"Great, I'll go get my weed from the truck," said
Ryan, as he got up from the table.

"I'll meet you on the bus," I said. "Just let me
wash my plate."

As Ryan sat across from me and pearled a joint of
weed from the Golden Triangle, just up the road from
where we were staying, he went into detail about his
ex, how she left, and how that was why he was where
he was: cruising down the coast with his truck packed,
stopping as he pleased before arriving at his final
destination. I didn't need to ask where that was, but I
pretended to be surprised when he told me.

Tijuana: the place where people usually go for that
one thing.

When I brought up one of the town's infamous
brothels, of which I had only heard lengthy, illustrative
tales about, Ryan stopped me short. He smiled giddily.
Clearly, the brothel's reputation had preceded itself; so,
of course, that was where my new friend had his sights
set.

"Just trying to clap some cheeks and forget about
her, brother," said Ryan, licking the joint sealed shut
before handing it my way. He nodded, giving me the
honors.

"It's funny," Ryan went on, stretching back in his seat on the old school bus that had been converted into a hangout spot for this exact reason. "The places I've lived, in South America, that kind of thing is normal."

I gave him a skeptical glance.

"No, really. It's not like it is here," said Ryan, grinning as he watched me put fire to the joint. "It's part of their culture down there. They don't really think about it, and it's not a big deal, because everyone does it."

"What sucks, though," he went on, pausing momentarily as he took the joint from me, "is when you can *tell* that they don't want to be there. They might be kissing up on you, pulling you onto the bed, or whatnot. But you can feel that they don't want to be there right now. That can be hard."

"...I can imagine," I said. "Though I can't say I know what that's like. Still have yet to step foot in one."

"No?" asked Ryan, surprised as he took a heavy rip of the joint. "Well, it might sound stupid or whatever, but I would say you should try it. For me, it's like therapy. I don't do it often. But sometimes it's just what I need, to take the edge off. And man, does it work. It sort of keeps everything balanced, you know?"

"Sure," I said. "I can see that."

"The key," said Ryan, handing the smoldering joint back over to me. "Is to not fall in love with them. *That* can get you in trouble. Well, at least, eventually."

15

The art of Trying to Make it Last

"Y ou don't have to be an extrovert to do this," said Albe.

A digital nomad from Colorado, Albe had found her way into the world of hosteling because the life back home—the monotony of being in one place for too long, mainly—had grown stale, and she was seeking something more than just a stable place to be while punching the clock. At first, it was a nice hotel. But there, Albe realized the only people she was interacting with were the waiters who dropped off her food, or some old woman at the grocery store who had seen her there before and was feeling chatty. While my friend could talk to anyone about just about anything, she felt a distinct disconnect in what she wanted versus what she was getting out of the nomadic lifestyle.

From her single-bed hotel room, Albe ventured out into the wilderness, working on a farm in Washington. Though while satisfying those inherent desires of hers to be in nature, and to see through a process that made

139

something tangible, the farm life had lacked one thing: community. A sense of place among the people, and a way to access them. After a stint on the farm, Albe looked into the volunteer program and found a hostel in Santa Barbara that suited several of her needs, which, naturally, made her stay quite a bit longer than she had expected. And like for so many others, that decision led to a new life.

Since the hostel was centrally located near several beaches and bars, and it had a quaint common area with enough space to spread out and work, Albe made the place her home for almost a year.

"I found it easy, here, because the space allows you to work independently, but it also allows you to approach the person next to you," she said. "It creates that vacation-like atmosphere, while still giving you somewhere to get the work done."

Not all spaces are created equal, which can make balancing work and play an art in itself, especially for those who, like Albe, are classified as a digital nomad. With the way the place is constantly turning over, sometimes with quite the mix of interesting characters, it can be a tight rope to walk, knowing when to engage with the next new stranger, and, just as well, how to say no—or, at least display such dedicated focus on something menial that someone who might want to talk will instead leave you alone.

Griffin, who was also working remotely while traversing through Southern California, but decided to stay, once he had a taste of the hostel life, touched separately on what it takes to know what is good, versus what is necessary when it comes to getting the most out of one's travel experience, particularly in a hostel.

"It's a balancing act," said Griffin. "You want to be in a place where there are people around so that you have someone to hang out with, but you also need to get your work done."

That realization came from having tested the waters on different types of accommodations over the course of several months. After giving up his apartment back home, in favor of living on the road as a digital nomad, Griffin found himself at first in Mexico, living in a quaint studio apartment, not far from the beach. What he imagined, when booking the spot, was a place to have both: a cheap spot to live for a month, in a place that was exotic and full of new experiences. But what Griffin found, rather quickly, was that the isolated nature of his new accommodations was not worth the money he was saving.

He fled his apartment in Mexico before the month was up, and returned to that same hostel as Albe in Santa Barbara, knowing that he wouldn't have the same sort of privacy there, and would have to be disciplined when it came to saying no, as there would, sooner or later, be someone tugging at his sleeve, inviting him to come along *somewhere*. The duality of having such a stimulating or highly social place to work, with ambitious travelers always around, becomes just that: an artful balance, but Griffin learned, rather early in his time jettisoning from Santa Barbara to cities like Palermo and London, that, as someone who works remotely, there was a way to have both, so long as one was willing to branch out or be flexible with their accommodations—having enough money, of course, also helps.

"If you're going to be in hostels, you need to find a place where you can actually work and focus. If the hostel doesn't have that kind of space, maybe that's a good coffee shop nearby," said Griffin. "Or, if you're going to book out a furnished apartment for a month, you could always find a hostel nearby and stay for a few nights just so you have a chance to make connections."

All the movement, however, can be displacing, and I even found it difficult sometimes, trying to explain to someone, especially a stranger, where I was from.

The answer could have changed slightly, depending on how long I thought I had and how long *they* might be staying; even then, the person inquiring might not still totally understand *why* it came with some hesitation. Naturally, the easiest place to start is always one's place of birth, but with so many stops in between, and all that factored into the decision to be *there*, now, it felt rather unjust to explain where I had come from as one specific place, especially as I knew that I wouldn't even be *there* too long.

There are certain downsides to doing this: it's a balance, to be living out of a bag, wearing the same few outfits all the time, not seeing family and old friends for months or even years at a time, all while trying to keep close contact with those other vagabonds in different cities, states, countries, from a previous time, a previous life, and still yet trying to tell yourself—and them—that it won't be long until you see one another again, and that everything will be the same when you do.

And yet in as many ways as they can become distant or even disappear, the wanderers and fellow nomads who might have become friends along the way may soon begin to feel like family: the volunteers, the bosses, or even a few of those long-term guests who stick around enough for more than just the good times, forgoing sometimes their own future travels for more of *this*. They're the ones who make the minor hiccups or small inconveniences worth it, because of what they offer you each day: a sense of community. And especially as a backpacker, that is one thing you cannot put a price on.

Having frequented a few of the same hostels during my time on the circuit, that much became apparent each time they dropped what they were doing to stop and give me a hug once they saw me come through the door, as if we hadn't seen one another in months or even years, when really, it had hardly been a couple of weeks. Because, in that time, so much had changed *there*, even if so much had stayed the same — and yet, they seemed just as excited to hear about where *I* had been, and what I had seen, since I left, as they sat amidst a new crowd of people who were suddenly quite interested in who I was, and what I was all about.

Though between stops, it became almost like a game, trying to recall the faces I found myself trying to place with familiar-looking strangers; from where do I remember *you*, and who are you, anyway?

It is the newness of it all, moreover, which helps keep it fresh and invigorating, or at least enough not to be weighed down by the fatigue of it. The fatigue that can follow one like a shadow, finding ways to crawl into the day because you kept the night going a little too long by saying 'yes' when you could have just as easily looked past that person or ignored their subtle cue for conversation in the kitchen. It can, just as well, come down to the simple, albeit honest, mistake of stopping in the hallway to have a conversation with a certain guest, and suddenly it is past midnight.

Personal space can feel like a theory, and privacy can seem like a foreign concept in a place like this. But what hostels might lack in privacy and the allotment of personal space, they make up for in several other ways. The indelible ones, like the deep conversations with people from all over the world, getting to see just how people truly are, *just* people.

Placing them in a social setting may, moreover, be what brings out in them something innate in all humans: that desire and longing for connection. Having crossed paths a wide range of different individuals along the way, it came, then, as little surprise to see someone who might have been quite shy or reserved at first, become one of the most interesting or talkative ones in the group—they only needed to be given the chance, a reason to step out of their comfort zone for a few hours at a time.

Social activities, which many hostels host, are essential to unlocking that *thing* in people, as they provide a much different take on travel than the standard hotel or bed and breakfast. Group activities or small excursions, especially, are how you *experience* a place instead of simply seeing it, which, I presume, most people set out to do when they travel.

Whether that means getting good and wasted with a bunch of rambunctious blokes on a Tuesday night, introducing a group of foreigners to s'mores around the fire, or getting up before dawn to hike in the rain with a carful of exhausted backpackers just to see the sunrise over the ocean, the wide range of experiences offered at any hostel can vary immensely, and perhaps, if one is so lucky, that single experience might then spark a chain reaction, and for the rest of the week, you find yourself following around certain people, exploring the various parts of that place you came to see.

It is also not uncommon to see a guest being snatched up by one of the volunteers, who may have noticed something in that person that suggested they would be a good fit with the others, and, before long, that guest is put on the schedule, pulling shifts at the hostel—if for no other reason than to stop the bleeding on their holiday budget, or perhaps to simply enjoy somewhere rather than just passing through, *again*.

I cannot say I have not had my hand in trying to influence certain guests that it might be a good idea to stay at the hostel for a while, since they had no real set plans other than to *be there*. As it was for myself, the assimilation process might be slow, but then, all of a sudden, that new hostel volunteer became so comfortable with the role of being a part of the team that they were eagerly leading groups of new guests across town to experience something they might have stumbled upon, or have wanted to try—and slowly, their personality starts to seep through, and they become a fiber of the place, helping it maintain that lively energy that makes the operation so unique, and yet, enigmatic, at times.

Enigmatic in the way that something as enriching as this could be so inexpensive, accessible to anyone. And that is what makes them so confounding, for some. The folks who own the houses nearby and mosey on over, eventually popping their heads inside the hostel just so they can ask: *What is this all about, anyway?*

You might start with the standard definition, telling them that it's an affordable place for travelers to stay, with shared bedrooms and also private rooms available, but end up segueing into some story about how *you* ended up there, and now you sort of live there. Usually, the locals are taken aback, but certainly intrigued by the concept, saying they'll have to try it sometime, or suggest it for their son or daughter who likes to travel.

Perhaps they're only trying to placate you; maybe they're being honest, and have enough curiosity to take a chance on this *thing* that they've heard about but never truly seen or experienced on their own. Hostels, like anything, must be experienced to be truly understood. And yet, the experience is not for everyone. Whether the individual realizes it after their first night, or while being guided on a tour during check-in, they might see that it is not for them, after all —and that's quite alright. Perhaps that person was expecting something a little different when they made their reservation. Sleeping in a room full of strangers is also not for everyone, I suppose.

Not everyone, moreover, is cut out for the lifestyle. A few of my friends in different cities or from my stops along the way have a hard time understanding *why* I continue to live the way that I do, teasing me about how infantile or even impossible it seems to them to be so indifferent to a few of the downsides of always being on the move and never quite knowing what's next. Yet, the longer that it has prevailed, the more they've sort of come to understand it, and will now merely chuckle as they ask where it is that I am in the world today.

While this path has rewarded me in ways that I could never truly define or put into text, it bears acknowledging that the toll of being like a discarded newspaper swept up by the wind, at times getting stuck on some foreign object along the way, before drifting to the next destination, *has* come at something of a cost. By now, I have lost track of many of the possessions lost along the way.

Whether lifted out of an unlocked room, left tucked under some bed sheets because I had an early plane or train to catch, or even forgotten on a city bus, the more I have lost throughout my travels, however, the less I came to actually care about how much it once cost or what it took to get it How I reached an upshot of almost complete indifference toward most material goods is better saved for another book, but at the same time, it now makes sense how easily adaptable this lifestyle has become, as living in hostels seems rather like just one more step forward in freeing oneself from all the *stuff*.

While certain items I might like to have back, I am able to laugh, just as well, at that almost unhealthy apathy I have developed toward the *stuff*, especially when realizing that I am wearing someone else's socks, but knowing just as well that that is only payback, since the dyer had already eaten so many of my own already, and, at least the ones I am wearing sort of match—in fact, they're actually kind of cool.

Life, it seems, is a lot smoother when you learn to let go. Things tend to come back around if you're patient enough. Patience is essential, especially in a place like this, one that is constantly changing and sometimes noisier than one would prefer. Whether that means learning to forgive some new acquaintance for their idiosyncrasies or annoying tendencies that are perhaps nothing more than that person's best effort to be themselves, or whether that means being fine with waiting for something that someone else happened to need at the same time as you, being in a place like this without practicing some degree of patience can be quite challenging.

The simple lessons in life, like being patient and exuding humility, tend to be unearthed in a place like this, even if those are not at first realized as being a requisite to the experience.

My friend Nikole, as she was preparing to make a pivot from the hostel industry after managing one in San Francisco for more than two years, sat down with me one day to expound on some of the many things she learned in her time in the industry.

"When I got here, I needed to learn so many things about human beings. How everyone is pretty much just the same, but we force ourselves to be blind to that," said Nikole. "It forces you to be humble. To lower your standards in the way that you should look at everybody, expecting nothing. Because at a hostel, you might have someone with a lot of money who can pay for a hotel. Or, you might have someone who is scraping quarters together for their stay. And yet those people have *nothing* that makes them different, so I need to treat them the exact same."

The things my friend picked up in her time, whether that was sitting behind the desk or exploring the city, leading activities and getting to know the locals, went beyond just learning about people through the constant observation of them—Nikole even added how it was a guest from another country who taught *her* about the lineage of her country, Brazil, in another continent.

Of the many things that make hostels so unique from other forms of accommodation while traveling is how one does not have to leave the common room, kitchen, or even get up from their desk to be able to get a taste or glimpse of the world. It comes to them. Sometimes several times within a single hour.

16

Things Easily Forgotten

I n the final writing stages of this book, I called my friend Albe and told her that it was nearly done, all those months later. She happily agreed to read the book, but, not more than a day later, called me to explain all the things that I had forgotten.

"How could you have left *this* out? Or *that!?*" she demanded, perplexedly. "There's so much meat left on the bone, Zack!"

Albe was right. I had forgotten several characters —some were intentionally left out, while others were simply displaced from memory due to the constant movement and inability to remember who was where and when. Albe made it a point to remind me of one individual, an old gentleman who caused so much trouble at the hostel that he needed to be reprimanded for his bad behavior.

It's sort of an unwritten rule *not* to sleep naked in shared dorms, and even more so frowned upon to stand in the window each morning and stretch, completely naked, while the others in the room stirred about, as this old man so casually did. The fellow made such a habit of it, moreover, that practically each morning a new guest would come to the front desk and complain. An awkward conversation, to say the least, needed to be had between him and the manager; finally, his behavior stopped, and he began wearing clothes to bed.

Of course, such an instance is quite rare, but not necessarily unheard of, given how easy it is to become comfortable in a place like this, and how natural it can be for someone to overstay their welcome, especially when it can feel like a hidden gem for them. Whether that's old or young, with how unique the setup is, and how seamlessly one can slip into its comforts, it's not particularly surprising to see certain guests abuse the leisures of a hostel. It can be, as Albe described it during our call, like a childhood experience: a sleepover that forever plays out. The regulars can become, as Albe added, like a piece of furniture that you just expect to be there whenever you get home.

"Don't you remember?" Albe pressed me as we rehashed some of the funny, absurd moments and people we encountered during our time working together. "How once all the old people checked out, the vibe changed completely? When all the young people came, it was like a completely different hostel!" Albe didn't stop there, insisting that I should write an entire chapter on this specific dynamic of old versus young travelers, and how that can be a very real part of hosteling that one might not necessarily expect when booking.

With my mind racing down memory lane, I then reminded her of the story about the one guest whom I checked into the hostel one night but who, by the next morning, was put on the blacklist and barred from ever returning. I had a strange feeling about him during the check-in process, as he appeared a bit intoxicated, but the fellow was sober enough to coherently answer all of my questions, and managed to check off several of the prerequisite boxes for guests, such as being from out of town and having proof of onward travel.

But his story was a classic example of how quickly things can spiral for a guest in a matter of hours. That buzz he had going, moreover, had escalated rather quickly after checking in, and he had caused something of a scene that evening, but it wasn't until the morning that he earned his last strike. Albe called me as I was down the road getting coffee, explaining that she might need me to come back and be the one to ask the man to leave, since he had thrown up in the bathroom at breakfast and not bothered to clean it or tell anyone.

"Of course," I said to Albe apologetically. "It's my fault he's there anyway. Let me know if anything escalates. I'll happily come back and kick him out. Just say the word."

"Thanks, I think I can handle it. But I will," she said.

About an hour later, I came back to the hostel. Albe intercepted me before I even made it through the door, laughing as she put her hands on my shoulder and explained what happened in the short time that I was gone.

"So," she said. "Our friend left. I told him at checkout that he needed to leave and was not allowed to rebook because of his behavior. But I did not know that *this man* decided to do his laundry right as it was time to check out. I told him, 'Fine. Finish your laundry. But then you must leave.' And then!" Albe exclaimed, pausing to chuckle. "When I got to the room to start stripping beds, he was still in there! I told him, 'Sir. It is eleven o'clock. You need to leave now. Or I will have to call the police.' Well, he didn't like that. So he started throwing a tantrum, kicking holes in the ceiling, and calling me a bitch. Thankfully Kai was there, so she threw him out. And now he's banned. So...there's that."

While difficult and sometimes stressful in the moment, it's the characters and instances like that which can make the whole experience so interesting on a day-to-day basis. And then, of course, there are the regulars, as Albe so reminded me during our call, who make it even that much more of a unique arrangement, with the way they come and go but still remain as a consistent part of the experience.

"The regulars *need* a chapter," she insisted. "You need to talk about the types of guests you get at a hostel and how they are all so *different*. You get the overnight guests with whom you might make no connection. Then you have the guests who are there for three days, maybe a week. Those are the people you get closer with," Albe explained. "Then you have the guests who are there for the full 14 days. They become such a big part of your reality. You get to know their habits, their schedules, their quirks. *And then*, you've got the people who come for a night or two every couple of months, and you build a different relationship with them, too. And then! And then you might have the yearly travelers who you see once or twice a year, and they become like your calendar. Those are the people who make you reflect on where you are and what's changed since you saw them last. You need to write about this, Zack."

Albe was correct—those characters and the sometimes chaotic moments made for good stories, and they even had a way of establishing certain eras or phases at the hostel. That unique dynamic creates some level of permanence to a place, and makes it feel, at least at times, like home, even if that home is constantly changing and its energy can be altered at the drop of a hat.

There might even be a guest who becomes like that old relative, coming in for a few days at a time with gifts, groceries, or gets down on their hands and knees to fix some broken appliance without being asked or it even being suggested. Uncle Joe was one of these individuals in Santa Barbara—we referred to him as *Uncle* Joe because he *was* a lot like that Uncle who was just as apt to critique something at the hostel as he was to bring snacks or a whole bushel of fresh vegetables from his garden for the staff to enjoy. The dynamic with Uncle Joe was different with everyone, and not all the staff members particularly loved his company, but Uncle Joe's altruism and his genuine appreciation for the facilities made you feel like it *was* worth the extra little attention and care, even if the common overnight guest might overlook something he pointed out that needed to be fixed or swept, or that you, too, might be gone soon.

17

The Efforts to Make it Last

There *is* this thing called money, which can either allow the experience to continue on for months or even years, or force it to end rather abruptly. That can be a hard lesson to learn, but it is especially important to keep in mind when budgeting for a trip or planning a stint as a volunteer somewhere new.

Volunteer programs at hostels tend to range in the number of hours required, but typically offer at least enough flexibility in the schedule for one to find something secondary, a side gig to supplement all the fun, or to procure some of the finer things along the way. If landing remote work or living off an old nest egg is not possible, hopefully, there is some sort of work to be found around town.

In fact, I've seen fellow volunteers make it look quite easy, landing a second or even third job in town and then parlaying that into an apartment down the road, and perhaps, in the same span of time, falling in love with a local. And then just like that, they're gone, and the next time you talk to them, it doesn't sound like they're planning to leave anytime soon. The town they came to see on vacation suddenly becomes home, and, had you asked them, that would have been the furthest thing from what they expected when they first signed up for the program.

As someone who has embodied something of a spontaneous approach toward traveling, seizing opportunities to tact at the first sign of a shift in wind, I have consequently found myself in situations where I was riding it down to the studs, doing all that I could to sustain the experience, but understood, just as well, that the possible gains from more of it meant a lot more than what I saw reflected in my bank account. No matter how far out one plans or saves in advance, money *does* make the experience go, but it may also serve as a simple reminder as to what is truly necessary, when it comes to the things you have, and the things you do not, other than the experiences at hand.

I found myself in Santa Barbara, between jobs and threading the needle to such a fine degree that things were starting to get a little strenuous. I was on a walk one day, just as dusk was starting to set in, and came to a point where I had to decide whether to go left or right. Suddenly, what I thought I saw out of the corner of my eye was something glimmering in the street, butted right alongside the curb. The road was empty, and so I trotted over to where it was and picked it up.

In my hand was some poor guy's wedding band. A ring, made of 13-carat gold, which fit snug around my finger. I looked quickly over both shoulders, saw no one, and then slipped the ring into my pocket. Dumb luck of mine, it seemed, but even more perplexing was that this exact instance had occurred to me before, when I was, quite similarly, under lean times, several years back, in a different city.

Unlike that first wedding ring I found lying in plain sight, however, I hardly considered keeping this one. It didn't feel like it was mine to keep, anyway, so I decided to go straight to the nearest jeweler once they opened the next day and have it scrapped for cash. On my walk back to the hostel, I thought of how long the sum could keep some wind in my sails, or perhaps how I could put it toward another train ticket, somewhere else.

But when I returned to show my friends at the hostel what I had found, more than one of them said to me, "You know that's a sign, right?"

I blushed, my mind immediately going to that guest I had been crushing on, in just the other room, and how it might not be so crazy, after all, to ask them.

"I think it's just good luck," I said, brushing them off.

"I don't know, Zack. People fall in love in Santa Barbara all the time. Maybe you're next," one friend replied, winking as they put away the dishes.

Going through my head, then, was how many staff members and previous guests I had seen fall under the spell, under that very roof, and then whisked away together, full of love, hope, and hardly a concern about the possibility that it was, after all, merely good timing. The idea of a bright new beginning was infectious with that piece of gold in my pocket, but the direness of my bank account overrode any notion of keeping it, for when that time *did* come.

One does not, however, have to put up with such extremes while doing this, taking a few bones as they are tossed, just for more of *this*—I may have simply read too much Henry Miller. Yet, one of the best things about hostels *is* the money they allow one to save, whether that person chooses to take part in the volunteer program for a bit, or whether they stay bouncing between hostels, sometimes booking one for three days at a time as opposed to one, since it can be cheaper that way. No matter how or when one decides to move, there are small perks that come with the transient nature of the space, such as the things left behind.

Do this long enough, like my friend Kai, and you'll find there are certain hacks to be had in hostels, such as: when the best time of day is to scavenge the guest fridge or go rummaging through the 'free box' for any old names and checkout dates. And then, before you know it, you might have just procured a full meal out of what has been left behind, even if it is a bit unsightly or still sort of cold on the inside, and, if you're willing to take chances, the findings can be pretty good. It's only a matter of time, then, before you start to ignore expiration dates or the big bite marks on that leftover breakfast burrito.

"Just eat around it," they'd say to me. "Besides, it's better than throwing it away."

Or, another common one was, "Well, if you don't eat it, I will."

You might find yourself, just as well, standing in the kitchen at just the right moment, and that person you befriended over breakfast or on a bar crawl the night before has a flight to catch, so there's no way they can bring that stick of butter, opened jar of peanut butter, or even that slab or wild-caught salmon—and they turn to you, asking if you would eat it.

"And how about a bag of weed?"

"Excuse me?"

"Well, since I'm getting rid of stuff, would you smoke this bag of *weed* if I left it?"

Even if you do not yourself smoke, it's usually not hard to find someone who does.

The further one eases into this way of living, however, the harder it can be to remember what it was like doing things the *normal way*, and perhaps easier to convince oneself why they left it behind. That can be a spacious apartment, a person, a good-paying job—the things that *other* people have, and seem to be quite happy that they do.

Doing this long enough, it has become just as apparent that we so often want what we can't have, but, at the same time, what's right for someone else is not necessarily right for us. The important thing—as cliché as it may sound—is to do the thing that calls to *us*, and not put too much stock into what someone *else* is doing, because there's a good chance that they are envying what *you* are doing, and would trade something in their life to have it, even if it's only for a little bit.

For some folks that I've met along the way, the dream was merely to go out and do it; for others, it was to never go back to how things *used* to be. As it goes for the latter, living this way, with such minimal expenses, but a plethora of rich experiences always waiting, can make it seem almost as if you've found a way to cheat the system—a side road to help you avoid getting stuck in that rut of paying rent but never really getting the most out of the place you're living, because of what it costs to maintain living there in the first place.

But no lifestyle is free of at least a few compromises. While they are unique to the individual, someone who has done this for a while will surely tell you that there *are* trade-offs, that it is not sustainable to live this way forever—to be constantly anticipating the next interesting thing because it's bound to walk through the door, tomorrow; to be always available, since there are so few places to hide; to somehow always be just a little bit behind on sleep, since simply saying 'no' can seem be quite difficult sometimes.

The unique setup of hostels, however, and how their dynamic can microwave so many of the good feelings but also pressure-cook some of the bad, only enhances the importance of remaining present throughout the experience, no matter how short or long it might last. That constant spin cycle of emotions and new faces that a hostel can offer, moreover, is what bears the revelation that so much of life *is* temporary, and such a notion can be rather important to remember when things are tough, or when they seem too good to be true.

Instead of dwelling on the imminence that it will all be over, eventually, it's much more advisable to appreciate the places and the people, for who they are and how they are each arranged so differently, rather than getting wrapped up in the things that make the situation imperfect or feel eternally fleeting.

18

A few Leftover Characters

A ge should never stop one from seeking knowledge, chasing love, or trying new things. Hostels, with all of their interchangeable components, have a way of exemplifying how there are always things to pick up along the way, even if one assumes that they already know quite a bit already or have been through enough for two lifetimes for something significant or profound to not even register as a blip on their radar.

I had met many travelers who had just turned 18 years-old and suddenly had their whole world opening up, having discovered places like *this* exist all over the world—and, just as well, heard a guest who was more than twice my age open up about the adversities in life while sharing a meal they had just prepared for myself and a few others, saying they were simply glad to have found such a place and now be surrounded by such interesting company.

That same traveler, who might appear a bit out of place amongst the young backpackers, but has come with oversized luggage of life experience, and perhaps a parcel of tips on how to survive it, is, just as well, worth getting to know. Perhaps, even more.

For me, John was one of those people. He showed up to the hostel like many others before him—not sure what to expect, but open to the idea, especially since it was a fraction of the price of a hotel just down the street, and the facilities were clean. John was the oldest person at the hostel when he checked in, and by the time he left, but, being generous and incredibly social, John fit into the hostel as well as any nomadic traveler, and connected with several guests and staff members during his stay. As I got to know John, I learned that he had been through a lot, especially right up to arriving at the hostel, but was as persevering as ever, and determined to get back to what had become a rather interesting career path.

Spotting talent was one of John's natural gifts, and he used that to help young ladies land gigs singing the National Anthem in sports stadiums around the country. A niche gig, something that might get overlooked by the people in the stands who just came to watch a ball game, but for many of the young women, it was their dream to sing on big stages, and having someone like John in their corner helped them get closer to that goal.

Somewhere along the way, John had met a young woman named Samantha who was a gifted singer, but Samantha had other talents. Years before she and John crossed paths, Samantha had written a children's book, which was, by all accounts, a solid book with a strong message. But the publishing industry is, like many creative industries, a tough one to crack. Although Samantha's book had been published and made available worldwide, it had not picked up much traction. Her book came up in conversation one day, and after Samantha showed John the book, he offered to help her get it into more hands.

John became, by default, Samantha's publicist, and it wasn't long before he was taking big swings with the book, making media contacts, and writing letters about how it deserved to be read. One of those letters went to the White House, to the President's wife, who was impressed with the book, and selected it out of more than a thousand children's books just like it, to be promoted around the country.

As the story goes, Samantha's book became a best-seller, because John had seen something in her—in it—and believed it needed—just like the other young women he worked with for landing singing gigs—to be seen. The success of Samantha's book, and how her and John's paths crossed for one purpose but wound up leading to something completely different and unexpected, felt like a microcosm for life—in how determination and believing in one's self are necessary things to remember and channel, in any endeavor—but also for the hostel itself, being that you never truly know who will come into your life at any given moment, and how a lone interaction can spark something much greater than you ever imagined.

As with business endeavors, romance can come down to a matter of timing. 'Right person, wrong time' can feel all too true to the lifestyle, since, quite often, the best part of the experience—the people—is always on its way out the door.

But for as many intense flings or hot pursuits in hostels that have ended because of sheer timing, countless others have flourished because of it—Sara and Tolga were a perfect example of that, and, even having watched it unfold in real time, from the first few days Sara showed up to the hostel in San Diego, to the very last, when we all said our goodbyes, I shouldn't have been, but still was, surprised at how quickly she and Tolga fell for each other.

"Wow, that happened fast," she said to me, a few days before packing her bags to leave, with Tolga, in their rented sports convertible, out to one of those iconic chapels in Las Vegas to say 'I do', before starting anew, albeit somewhere that was yet to be determined. Those four months went by fast, Sara said, to which I solemnly agreed.

"I have to say," she chuckled. "This was *not* what I expected when I signed up to do the volunteer program here. I wonder what my parents will say. That is, if I even tell them."

Love stories like the one between Sara and Tolga are astonishingly common in a place like this, but it doesn't always have to be a physical attraction or feeling of affection that one finds at a hostel, which makes them compelled to stay. Sometimes, it's simply the company or the comforts a place that was supposed to merely be a stopover.

Theo, a professor from Brazil, was just passing through Santa Barbara on his way to Central America, and was like Sara: pleasantly surprised by this *thing* that he had just found at the hostel. Like my friend in San Diego, Theo had not anticipated sticking around the same area for several months, but had seen enough in his first week there to know that *this* was different.

A somewhat rare example of a guest who went from a staff favorite to being one of the staff, Theo was a fellow who had just as much passion for his cleaning duties at the hostel as he did sharing his thoughts on a litany of highly introspective matters with the guests and other volunteers. Theo, as it happened, also liked to get high and would tease me, saying, "I am the devil on your shoulder," with a cheeky grin and a fresh jar of exotic weed on his way to the school bus, nearly every morning.

I was usually in the middle of some project, and tried to brush him off each time Theo would offer me to join him on the bus. But it became rather difficult the more time I spent around him, and I got to see just how much he knew about life, language, and the world, and I realized how I had a great deal to learn from him. So what was I *supposed* to do?

For hours, Theo and I would sit in that old yellow school bus that had been converted into a smoking lounge and talk about literature, philosophy, different cuisines and customs around the world, trading music selections while we toked it up. Theo's bandwidth for information was as impressive as his ability to smoke throughout the day and still be quite articulate and function at a high level. It came as little surprise, then, to hear how, instead of reading the material for one of his recent lectures back home, before coming to America, Theo sat in his bathtub with three fat joints and listened to several podcasts on the subject. The lecture was, of course, a smashing success; naturally, his students loved him, as so many of the staff and guests at the hostel did.

A rare individual in a lot of ways, Theo was an asset to the hostel during his time there, and his decision to stay for a while proved how special the place could be at any given time, and yet how so much of it may come down to sheer timing.

At times, it can feel like you've just been put in charge of hosting a family gathering, with the way the house fills up with people overnight, after having been nearly empty for several days. Suddenly you find yourself playing host, making sure someone doesn't get too out of hand or that there is enough ice in the cooler; or, hoping perhaps that when you do run into that person you don't want to talk to, someone sees and comes over and drags you away, maybe to where the real party is: into the kitchen, onto the deck, around the fire, down by the beach.

Then, all of a sudden, *that* place becomes like its own party, and then, in *that* new assortment of people, you may strike up a conversation with someone that's more interesting than they let on; and perhaps that is when you hear something that you needed to hear for a while now, but just needed a fresh voice to say it, someone that had no attachment to you beyond the fact that you just met and are both sharing this *thing*. Perhaps now you're ready to try that thing you were reluctant to do: to visit that country you've heard and thought so much about, to talk to that cute guest you noticed giving you eyes from across the room when they checked in, to call that friend you've been thinking about but have been avoiding because you know how the conversation is going to go.

The people, I can only presume, are what keeps most of us hooked on it—the lifestyle exposing one to a litany of characters who could probably warrant their own book; a collection of moments and conversations that make it hard not to think that *this* was what was missing the whole time, even if that can seem almost impossible to fully explain, and even more difficult to capture again.

And, sometimes, there are, along the way, those strange interactions that make you wish that you had just a bit more time to act on that *feeling*.

Katrina had been at the hostel for a few days, and while I had found her to be quite attractive, it wasn't until her last day that I actually said something to her.

Katrina was working on a craft project at the desk next to me, and something I had overheard her say to someone else prompted me to ask her about her next stop. We got to talking, and amongst the art and the travel, I asked about the stack of tarot cards on her desk.

"Have you ever had yours read?" she asked.

"Actually, no. I've always been a bit worried about what I'll find out."

Katrina grinned and then reached over to her pile of cards, giving them a quick shuffle.

"Ahh," she said slowly, peeling a card from the top of the deck and placing it down for both of us to see.

"The Fool." She smiled, hinting that perhaps she knew something I did not.

"What does that mean? Is it bad?"

"Well..." said Katarina. "It's upright, so that can mean a few things." She paused, looked at me, and then said softly and slowly, but with confidence, "You're entering a new chapter in life, aren't you?"

I froze up. "Actually, yeah. I may have just landed a new client for another writing project. So, I think that adds up..."

Katrina smiled at me again. "Good. Well don't be afraid. Go forward with it," she said. "Even if you're not sure where it will go. This is a chance to forge a new path. There could be something down the road for you."

My heart flickered for a moment. I sat back in my seat and watched as the girl casually went back to her project, suggesting that our session was over.

"That's good advice, I'll remember that," I said. "Well, now that you know that about me, what about you? What's in your cards?"

Katarina looked up from her art project and looked at me, saying airily, "Oh, I'm the devil."

Somehow, I believed her, and yet, now I wanted to get to know this mysterious girl even more than I had when she first arrived—only, it was nearly eleven o'clock, and Katarina had a train to catch.

Although nothing transpired from that moment, it serves as a reminder that—as important as it is to *seize* it—any good story can start with a hello. That lone introduction might then be why someone opts to stay in a certain place for months on end, working as a volunteer or looking for apartments in town since the idea of leaving suddenly seems so hard, as having such an abundance of interesting people around was not necessarily not an expectation of theirs when booking a bed in a shared dorm room halfway across the world.

It's no surprise, then, to walk by a bulletin board in the lobby of a hostel and see the hand-written love letters from previous guests or volunteers, professing the impact of the place on their personal life, and promising that they will, at least one day, be back.

Ant was one of those characters who made himself known from the moment he set foot in the hostel. I remember watching him, as I sat in the lobby, working on my laptop, gazing around the sunlit hostel with an eager gleam in his eyes. The girl at the desk asked Ant to repeat himself after he had listed the name on his reservation. Antoine Martine Archambeau was a lot to remember, to be sure, and Ant could tell by her expression that she had already forgotten it after he repeated it for the second time.

"Eh, you can just call me the French guy," Ant chuckled, as he grabbed his bags and followed the receptionist on her tour of the hostel.

The beach hostel in Santa Barbara would be his home for the next two weeks while he waited for his student housing down in Isla Vista to open up, and it appeared, by the look on Ant's face that afternoon, that he was pleased with his decision. For far more than the standard 14 days, Ant would become quite the talking point at the hostel; a character with a genuine zeal and curiosity for life, Ant took quite easily to the modern conveniences of American living, getting rather comfortable with all of the distractions and easily engrossed with all of the different people and ways to unravel a day.

Since we all enjoyed his company, and he was generous with many of the libations and party favors he brought out onto the sunny patio practically every single afternoon, Ant slowly became entrenched as one of *us*. An honorary guest who would regularly be invited to dinner with the staff, and even be given certain liberties when it came to doing laundry past quiet hours, using the staff fridge for his beer, or occasionally bringing in an outside guest to the hostel for an afternoon—while he embodied many of the best attributes of a hostel guest, Ant was not the typical hostel guest.

That leeway we gave him, however, became a slippery slope, and, as it had with several others before and after him, too much of a good thing became a bad thing. Ant became so comfortable—too comfortable—that he went from bending certain rules to flat-out breaking them, sometimes taking extra grace on things that would otherwise not be acceptable for guests, such as fighting with another guest in the kitchen at 3 a.m.

What happened that night was, however, less of a fight and more of an ass-whooping laid on another guest. Unbeknownst to the guy who picked a fight with Ant after the two of them went to a college party out in the hills together, Ant was trained in Brazilian boxing and had such quick instincts that the "fight" was over before it even started.

A few other staff members and I watched in awe the next day, the camera footage that was captured in the kitchen the night of their fight. While we couldn't hear the audio of what was said or how it was said, what we watched unfold was an almost unbelievable sequence.

Ant and the guest had apparently been arguing since they had left the party together, and something was said in the heat of the moment that prompted the guest to give Ant a shove. Ant shoved him back, prompting the guy to suddenly reach into the wooden block of kitchen knives and pull one out. Before the knife even came out of its sheath, Ant sent the guy a right hook and sent him tumbling to the ground.

Whereas most guests would be immediately thrown out for knocking out another guest, Ant was given something of a pass for the tussle. The other guest, who clearly escalated the situation by pulling out a deadly weapon, was promptly asked to leave the hostel and banned from ever returning. When the guy tried to plead his case, all the manager had to do was bring up the footage of the fight, and then that was that.

While Ant may have received a pass, he was put on probation after that. No more shenanigans, or you're out, he was told. That sudden burst of violence seemed, however, out of character for Ant, who was jovial and otherwise kind in spirit. Ant felt bad, of course, and understood that he was walking on thin ice from that point on, but that didn't necessarily stop him from pushing certain boundaries.

A week or so later, Ant and a few guests went out again. Tony, a previous volunteer, was among the group, and Tony, like Ant, took certain liberties with the staff despite the fact that he no longer worked for the company and was simply another paying guest at the time. Tony went on a bar crawl with the hostel guests that night, accompanied by an old buddy named Chris. Both Tony and Chris were nice guys, but there was immediately bad blood between Ant, Chris, and Tony. Part of that stemmed from Ant having his eye on one of the young, attractive foreign backpackers who came along on the pub tour, and, as it so happened, Tony had similar interests.

What transpired that night became, largely, a game of 'he said, she said,' and, while there were a few other guests who bore witness to the event, it was difficult for anyone who was *not* on the pub tour to discern truth from embellishments. The embellishments seemed about as bad as they could be—Tony, who came to the staff later the next morning, claimed that Ant was taking advantage of the female backpacker. But to Ant, it was mutual, and he and the girl were as smitten with one another as they were intoxicated. When things came to a head—according to one of the other guests—it was when Ant brought the girl back to the dorm and decided to treat the shared space like a private room.

Naturally, this was grounds for *anyone* to be kicked out of the hostel. For Ant, it was the last straw, and, no matter how much he pleaded his case, insisting that he and the girl were sober enough to know what they were doing, the manager had no choice but to cancel the rest of his reservation and refuse him from ever rebooking. There was confusion, anger, and a good deal of resentment from Ant, especially considering that Tony was not supposed to be responsible for making such decisions, but had been successful in swaying the staff and even friends of Ant's to get him shunned for his actions.

The energy of the place, once Ant left, had shifted. It was strange not seeing him outside each afternoon, sitting around the fire pits, talking with different guests, cracking beers or sharing a smoke with one of the volunteers; his presence was the kind that you missed only once it was gone, and made you realize how unique the dynamic at a hostel can be when there are inquisitive, adventurous and otherwise amicable backpackers who decide to stay for longer than just a few days. And even though he was gone, Ant gave us plenty to talk about as we sat around the dinner table and shared our staff meals together.

Flash forward a few months, and Ant's time in the States was coming to a close, and he would have to return to France to return to reality. In a last-ditch effort, Ant reached out to me, asking if he could come back to the hostel for one last goodbye, since he still felt guilty about how things ended so sourly after starting off so well. Somewhat reluctantly, the hostel manager agreed, and so not an hour later, there was Ant, with a bottle of bubbly wine tucked under his arm and a big smile on his face, standing in the doorway of the hostel.

"Ahh, it feels good to be home," he said as he popped the bottle of wine and began pointing around the lobby, asking anyone if they would like a glass. Ant gazed around the sunlit room, taking a deep breath. "This place meant a lot to me. It was my home." He put a hand on his chest. "You guys were my first American friends. It wouldn't be right without being able to say goodbye. Even if things, eh, did not end so well."

Amends were eventually made as Ant was able to relay *his* side of the story, but not without apologizing for his propensity to push the boundaries so often with us. "I got carried away," he admitted. "I understand why things happened the way they did. And I am sorry."

But perhaps what makes Ant's impression on the hostel, and this story, especially noteworthy, and even a bit ironic, is that, between the time Ant was kicked out of the hostel and returned to give his apologies, Tony was temporarily banned from the hostel for his own bad behavior. Like Ant, Tony had gotten a bit too carried away with his liberties at the hostel, and one night wound up projectile vomiting all over one of the shared dorms after returning from a bar crawl, earning him a spot on the blacklist for any of the hostel properties for several months.

19

Some of the Stops
Along the way

PORTLAND, OR

It was, I presume, the guy who tried three different keys to get into the dorm until finally getting the right one to work, who woke me up at 2:27 a.m. when he stumbled into the room. These things happen; people spend the night at a hostel for no other reason than to experience the nightlife there. That, I did not hold against him. What transpired next, however...

It was around 3:30 in the morning, after having gone back to sleep, that I was awoken rather abruptly by another sound. A low rumbling fart—also not uncommon in a shared dorm room—but the sort that left a sad, pitiful feeling in the air. The fellow above me, from whom it came, suggested as much by the way he groaned and then began noisily wiping his bed sheets in agony. It sounded like he made quite the mess.

Staring at the bottom of the bunk with my eyes wide open, a bewildering, 'are you fucking kidding me' sort of smirk came over me. *This* was certainly a new one for me. And I wondered, at that moment, mostly out of curiosity, if anyone else in the room had heard what happened, and if they, too, were chuckling in their bed.

Not a moment later, a substance came trickling at my side. It sounded like water pelting a tin roof. Unable to believe it at first, I watched as the tiny drip marks splattered onto my sheets, and quickly realized that in its path was a cloth pocket that was attached to the wall, where my glasses, wallet, phone, and keys lay. The safest place in the room, naturally.

My arm shot over to where my belongings were stashed, and I yanked them away before rolling out of bed and tiptoeing to the door and shutting it.

Outside, in the hallway, in an almost drunk-like state of exhaustion, I leaned against the door and shook my head, trying to not only comprehend what was happening, but where to go from here. I was in my pajamas, but was certainly not about to get back into bed. I realized my hand may have also gotten slightly wet, but refrained from giving it a sniff in case it were to confirm that sick suspicion—it seemed better in the moment *not* knowing.

Since the hostel was a hybrid between a hotel, there was a girl working the overnight shift at the front desk in the downstairs lobby.

"Hello," she said, a bit startled to see me as I approached.

"Hi," I said, "Umm...I think I might need a new bed."

The girl smiled and then politely asked me which room I was staying in and why I was making this request at almost four in the morning. I let out a deep breath, and then, to the best of my ability, explained to her *what* had just happened, bewildering her with a few graphic details. The girl's hand went over her mouth as she held back her laughter.

Nodding on occasion as I tried to make it clear that I *understood* and was not mad, the girl listened patiently. It would be best, I concluded, that it not be brought up to the fellow, and we just pretend it never happened at all.

"I just want a new bed." I sighed. "I don't care what room it's in, just so long as it's not...below him. If that is even possible."

The girl, still in a state of shock, got right to work and quickly found me a vacant bed in the same room. It was the last one left all weekend—so I was lucky, in a sense.

"I'm sorry," she said again, still taken aback.

"It's alright. These things happen," I replied. "And for some reason, always to me…"

Once the matter was resolved, and she reserved a different bunk for me, I asked if I could stretch out on one of the couches in the lobby and try to catch at least an hour of sleep before the cafe next door opened up. That feeling of intoxication that comes from such little sleep was still hanging over me like a cloud, but I had plans the next day and had no intention of interrupting them for a little bit of lost sleep.

The receptionist quickly agreed and let me be. Several minutes later, though, it came to her. The girl left her desk to come over to explain what she thought happened.

"The guy above you, I remember when he came back late last night!" she exclaimed, seeming as excited as she was relieved. "He twisted his knee, so I gave him a bag of ice. It must have melted. That must be what it was, the liquid on your bed. If that makes you feel any better."

I smiled wearily. "Right. Well, can I still have a new bed?"

"Of course," she laughed, standing over me as I lay sprawled out on the couch. "Do you mind if I sit down?"

Her name was Emily, and we talked through the morning hours, not anymore about the mysterious liquid or the fellow in the bed above me, but instead about *her* town: Portland. It appeared, to most people, that it was in shambles. The pandemic had done a number on it, and downtown was certainly not the same. That much was obvious to anyone who had been there before and after.

"Like, I know it's messed up right now," said Emily. "But there are still so many great things about this city, and it upsets me that it gets overlooked by some of the problems it has."

Emily was a proud native—something that has become increasingly rare in a city like Portland—and expressed how the politics had a lot to do with *why* things had taken such a turn. According to Emily, the city at one point had put in barricades to stop people from sleeping on the sidewalks outside of businesses in affluent areas, but no sooner had to pay to have them removed since they were not up to code.

"Like, what the fuck are we actually doing?" she laughed, shaking her head in bewilderment.

It started to make sense why certain parts of the city were the way that they were, and moreover, why it was perceived the way that it was, especially by outsiders.

Later that day, while I was waiting for a friend to pick me up from the hostel, I sat in the same lobby, watching the people go by through large glass windows. Over my shoulder, I heard a conversation between two younger couples who had come in from out of town for a wedding. They were dressed well and seemed to be looking for somewhere to eat brunch.

I have a poor habit of eavesdropping, but especially in places like this, with such a wide range of people around and enough time on my hands. When it was explained by someone in their party that the boutique hotel they booked also doubled as a *hostel*— the very one I was staying at—their voices became hushed, as if they were ashamed of the fact, and did not want anyone within earshot to know this fact.

It was a shame, I thought, that they had truly no idea what the hostel actually had to offer, even for the ones who, like them, ostensibly had the means to travel extensively. So it became, in fact, rather funny, listening to them speak about it in their quiet voices, about how they had gone out drinking the night before, out on the town—except, in all of the wrong places. The trepidation and regret in their voices suggested they never left the central downtown area, and now, *that* was their lasting impression of the city.

Perhaps what perturbed me—more than the fact that those four travelers would probably never stay in a hostel, even one as nice as the hotel-hybrid one they happened to have chosen—was the thought that they would probably never come back to Portland, which seemed quite sad, given that the receptionist from the night before was right: Portland *was* a great city, and it had so much to offer, from a food and culture standpoint to its sheer natural beauty and places to get lost. It only required an open mind and willingness to go looking.

SOUTH BEACH - Miami, FL

A few weeks after my abominable train ride out to Los Angeles with Josh, I found myself on the East coast, moving slowly by rail down its steadying landscapes, first from New York, and then through Philadelphia and Baltimore, before winding up in Miami.

Taking my brother's advice on one of the hostels in South Beach, I booked the cheapest one I could find. He had sold me on the fact that they had great specials on drinks and even provided food for their guests—it was almost *too* cheap.

Since he hadn't steered me wrong yet, I booked the hostel my brother recommended without giving it a second thought. It wasn't until I checked on my reservation, however, while riding through the lush farms in rural Georgia, that I actually gave the place a look.

Starting with the most recent reviews, I gave the hostel's webpage a quick scroll, even though I was less than 24 hours out from arriving, so there would be no changing my reservation without being charged. I barely made it through the first few reviews before getting anxious; the testimonies were all, at best, abysmal.

The hostel sounded, frankly, like a living nightmare, and I immediately opened a new browser and booked the next cheapest hostel I could find, which was just down the road. After receiving a confirmation email, I wrote a quick email to the owner of the first hostel, giving them some lame excuse as to why I needed to cancel my reservation.

The owner promptly replied: Sorry, no refunds within 24 hours.

It was worth a shot, and the way I saw it, I was doing *them* a favor by not having to leave another bad review.

It was dark when I finally arrived at the train station. Having been on public transit for the previous 24 hours, I decided to call a car instead of transferring buses a few times to get to South Beach. Miami, as it so happened, was hosting Art Basel that weekend, another small detail I seemed to overlook while planning my trip.

When I woke up the next day, I was pleased with my decision to eat the cost for the first hostel. Like the one in Portland, the second hostel I booked was a hybrid between a hotel, so it had all the bells and whistles: a sprawling patio, a swanky cocktail bar on-site, dozens of lounge chairs surrounding a shallow blue pool, and beautiful women in string bikinis lounging about. Surely, I could have done worse.

My luck continued to turn a corner since getting burned on the first reservation, as a couple of the other guys in my room, Mark and Matt, seemed to be keen on becoming friends as soon as we shook hands and made our introductions the next day. Being from another Florida town, just up the way, the two friends regularly came down to South Beach to go clubbing, and immediately invited me out with them that night— of course, once we had all taken our naps.

Around the pool, several hours later, the three of us started planning out the night. The sprawling patio had, in the meantime, turned into a full-blown party, with a hired DJ mixing records and people splashing around in the pool. Nearly every seat in the place was filled by the time it got dark, and there was a line starting to form at the door. With the full bar being just steps away, we decided *this* was the place to be, at least for a while.

In the meantime, two Canadian backpackers sitting next to us had overheard Mark and Matt talking up the club scene in South Beach; the Canadians had heard stories about the American clubs but had never been inside one. From my new friends, the two backpackers were given a good bit of advice: bring your wallets.

"We went to one last night that was $250 just to walk through the door," said Matt.

The two backpackers couldn't believe their minds, doing the quick calculation to convert into Canadian dollars.

"That was for guys," added Matt. "Girls got a break. For them, it was only $200."

"But that's Miami, for you," said Mark.

Turning to my left, I noticed a pretty girl from Norway sitting next to me. As we made conversation, I got the sense that she was distressed, also shocked by how expensive everything in Miami was—like many foreigners before her, the question of "*why*" became unavoidable when it came to the price of things in America.

The girl wanted to know if I had recommendations for any other hostels nearby.

"Sure," I said, and then gave her the name of the hostel I had booked but cancelled on my ride down.

The girl shook her head, moaning, "No, no. I just came from there! That place is terrible—it was so bad that I cried!"

Absent any other options, I suggested she try the internet before excusing myself to the bar. It was a sleek setup with a pair of bartenders with neatly trimmed beards and matching Hawaiian shirts behind it, shaking cocktails. I knew right off the bat that my night was not going to be cheap, and yet, it also never pays to be cheap, so I chose a respectable tequila and said thank you as one of the bartenders handed me a stiff drink.

By the time I went back to the bar, they were out of the specific tequila I had chosen, so I went with a slightly better label.

"Fine choice, sir," said the bartender, proceeding to hand me another tall, fizzing glass. It was halfway through my second drink that Matt and Mark told the others that they were ready to hit the town, so I quickly finished it on my walk to the bar so that I could settle up. The bar had gotten quite busy, as had the rest of the hostel, and there seemed to be no hurry from anyone to leave. I wondered then if I could persuade my new friends to stay, instead of going to the clubs.

"One more, please," I called to the bartender, and then made a slashing gesture at my throat to suggest I was ready to quit.

The bartender smiled before disappearing. A moment later, he returned with a printed bill and my card.

"Tip is included. Have a good night," he said, and then turned to help out another guest.

Already anticipating a large sum, I had prepared myself for the shock. But the number on the slip was outrageous. I couldn't believe it. The much wiser decision, it seemed obvious now, was my original idea: to walk to the corner store, buy a bottle of fine tequila, and split it amongst the group. For the price of those three drinks, I could have instead bought *two* nice bottles for us.

I went back to where Matt, Mark, and the Canadians were sitting and, in a low voice, explained what had just happened, perplexed at my lack of oversight on such a minor detail: we were in South Beach, Miami.

Seeing that the small setback had me rattled, Matt clapped me on the back and leaned over to urge me to look into the sort of online work that he used to generate revenue while being on the move.

"There's tons of ways to make money online these days. It's almost too easy not to," said Matt.

I told him I would look into it, since it seemed he had the lifestyle to back it up, for from Miami, Matt was off to Guatemala. Then, perhaps Panama or Costa Rica. Whatever he felt like doing when it came time to make the decision.

I had just finished logging some hours for my remote gig when I saw a young man sitting alone in the courtyard outside of our room. I nodded at him, offering nothing more than an easy, "Hey, how's it going, man?"

A smile came over him. "Would you like to buy some weed?" he asked, without answering my question.

"Well, no," I began to say. "Actually...yes, I would."

He grinned, patting an open seat at the picnic table.

"But, I fly out tomorrow," I said, making my way over to him. "So, not that much."

The guy reached into his side pack and nodded his head.

"I could sell you a dub," he said, procuring a large nugget of plump green ganja before pulling out a plastic bag and a small scale.

I hesitated for a moment. "What about just a joint?"

He paused to consider, and then nodded again.

"Yeah, sure. That works."

As the fellow broke the weed down into a reasonable amount for a joint, which he then proceeded to roll, we talked about art, life, and the trick to making a little money on the road.

"Not a bad side hustle," I said, alluding to the ease of his operation.

He grinned. "Miami is expensive. Not like Texas."

From there, we got to talking about Austin, Southern California, and then a couple of the same places we had both frequented in our respective time traveling, wondering aloud if we had somewhere along the way crossed paths. It so happened that both he and I had been doing this for a while, bouncing around various parts of the country, trying out different lifestyles for a beat.

Without saying exactly what *he* did for money, the fellow proceeded to implore about my occupation.

"A writer of sorts," I told him. "You know, I have one of my books with me. I think it's my last one. Maybe I can put it toward...this. Since I might only have...twelve dollars on me."

He stopped what he was doing and looked at me, sneering.

"Wait, I might have the full fifteen on me. I just might need a minute to find it."

The guy began to laugh. "Sure, man. Go ahead."

After some digging, I plucked my last Susan B. Anthony coin that I had saved for occasions just like this one, and gathered a wad of crumpled bills for him. After counting it, I apologized, having come up two dollars short.

"I don't care, bro. I find this shit funny," he said, taking my book along with the cash and then handing over the joint for me to spark.

Once the joint was finished, the fellow stood up. "Alright, I've got to go. There's work to do. The clubs are starting to get busy."

VENICE BEACH - Los Angeles, CA

The plan was to meet Shannon over in Redondo Beach before my flight took off. An old friend of my brother's, Shannon, was born in Redondo, the small beach town in southern Los Angeles, and so she offered to show the two of us around, taking us to a few different haunts and showing off the various nooks and crannies where she and her friends spent nights under the stars, sipping whiskey and smoking pot.

Since at the time I considered myself adept at flying intoxicated, there was little hesitation in joining her and my brother as they split up the bottle of wine into several paper to-go cups and then found a secluded place where we could smoke the joint that she had rolled.

"The people here take it very seriously," Shannon urged, looking over her shoulder as she led us down a quiet alley. "They'll actually call the cops if they see you smoking. So we need to be careful."

From there, we found a stretch of sand and sat down, watching as the waves came crashing in, catching up on old times. Even more seasoned a traveler than my brother and I, Shannon was a vagabond in every sense of the word. She had been around the world and back, and had plenty of stories to back up her wild times in Thailand, and her harrowing treks through the Amazon with her and her boyfriend, who was presently in Vietnam, where she had just flown in from, before meeting us. Nomads like Shannon are the ones who will make any traveler feel like they haven't seen a sliver of the globe, not even sniffed the real world.

Before long, the wine was gone, and the sun was slowly drawing toward the shimmering ocean. I looked down at the time with the sinking realization that I would have to get ready to leave. Having burned through enough cash on many frivolous things along the way, I decided to take the bus to the airport, since it was not far, at least in LA terms.

A few side glances from the TSA officers as they watched me fumble through the scanners, and I was through security without any snags. I found a seat at my gate and plopped down, smitten with my ability to still execute the feat under such conditions. Seeing that I still had time to spare, I pulled out my phone to call an old friend to catch up.

But somewhere in the course of our conversation, my flight had taken off: without me. By the time I realized it, the small rectangular screen above the door of the gate was flashing the word SEATTLE, with a new departure time. My heart went to my throat, thinking that someone had made a mistake. Maybe they changed gates without making any announcement, I assured myself as I stood up and started walking toward the nearest kiosk. Without looking up from his monitor, the man working the counter confirmed my fears: the doors were shut, and the plane was preparing for take-off.

"Can't you get me on another flight?" I stammered.

The attendant sighed, looking up at me.

"Normally, we don't do this. You usually have to buy another ticket, but..." he said, hammering away at his keyboard for a moment, before producing in his hand a new ticket. "Your flight takes off on Wednesday morning," he said. "Try not to miss it this time."

"You're a life-saver," I said. "Thank you."

I took my bags and found somewhere to sit while I worked out a new plan. It was Monday, and I had to be at work on Tuesday morning; so the bosses were, of course, less than pleased to hear the news, but they understood things *do* happen sometimes.

"Someone will cover you. Don't let it happen again, and consider it a verbal warning," they said, before hanging up.

Up to that point, I had, as one does while traveling, spent quite a bit more money than I had expected to, and the thought of shelling out even a little more cash for another night at a hostel was certainly sobering. But LA, being the behemoth that it is, I was confident that I could find a cheap hostel near the airport. I sat on the ground with my bags, letting my phone charge in one of the sockets on the wall while searching for an empty bed for the night.

It didn't take long, and I quickly received a confirmation email for a hostel a few miles away. But it wasn't until I read the fine print that I realized that the hostel was, as the name had so indicated, an international travelers' hostel: *no Americans allowed.*

It was stated very clearly at the bottom of the email.

"We can make an exception this time," said the girl on the phone, after I had explained my situation, insisting that it was an honest mistake.

"Don't worry," she said. "We'll see you when you get here."

As incompetent as I felt, I considered myself to be quite lucky, because things could have just as easily gone the other way, as I would quickly learn once I began working at a hostel. Several times on a night reception shift, I received a phone call just like the one I had made that day, from someone who underestimated the length of their travels, or was perhaps experiencing some other unforeseen delay and was now desperately hoping that someone would be awake when they arrived to check them in. It might have gone against policy to leave a key outside for someone without verifying that person's identity, taking them at their word instead of screening them when they showed up, asking questions like:

Are you local? What is your next stop? Where are you coming from?

But having been in their shoes, I saw just how much the little things can make a big difference when those same travelers would come up to me at breakfast and thank me for being so k_nd or understanding on the phone. The small things do matter, and that's part of what makes the experience special, even if it is, at times, stressful.

HONOLULU, HI

The first time I showed up on the island of Oahu, I had just been living in Southern California, and naively thought that it couldn't get much better than that. I had heard stories from other backpackers about Hawaii, seen the stunning images of its waterfalls, jaw-dropping cliffs, and lush tropical foliage in magazines and on movie screens; I knew that it was somewhere people spent their whole year working to spend two weeks vacationing.

Bouncing around as much as I had, the idea of another beautiful place hardly registered as exciting, but, within moments of walking through the airport terminals in Honolulu, the island air quickly enveloped me, and everything seemed to slow down a bit. As I looked around, I realized that 'island time' was a real thing, as almost everyone else had slowed down, too, so it would be sort of weird not to follow suit.

But I wasn't like many of the other tourists there —I was not some high roller looking to spend my wad on the Waikiki strip. I was on a shoestring budget and had only booked the flight because my brother had been living on the island for a few months and bugged me each time we spoke about how I should already be there.

I could see why he had become so partial to Oahu, though. The island life had been good to him, and it was just my brother's luck to land work right away and wind up living on the 37th floor of a high-rise condo, simply because the guys who owned the unit liked his vibe and got the sense he'd be easy-going. It was, undoubtedly, a needle in a haystack, considering he could make his rent working a part-time job and still have a little beer money on the side.

Had he not spent the previous month working at a hostel down the street, however, it's hard to say my brother could have ended up in a place like *that*. A collision of dumb luck and impeccable timing, my brother's path was another classic example of how the volunteer program in hostels could be quite the springboard for someone looking to acclimate to a new, albeit rather expensive, area.

Having worked at one and stayed at several others in town, my brother gave me the inside scoop on which hostels in Waikiki to avoid and who to talk to at each one. Not five minutes into checking into the one he suggested, I bumped into a girl who had just come from Santa Barbara, and had been working at the hostel where I had just spent the last several weeks. We had never met but had heard of one another in passing, from people in the circuit. The more time I spent in the circuit, the more common such a thing became.

The hostel in Waikiki I had chosen, moreover, used its popular group chat to connect travelers at its sister locations, becoming a virtual place for backpackers to meet other backpackers and make plans; on any given day, there were people plotting out extravagant hikes and trips across the island together. Towards the end of my stay, I decided to take part in one of the many planned activities and signed up for one of the sunrise hikes at the Lanikai Pillbox Trail.

It was mere minutes into getting into the van that morning that I noticed one of the girls next to me wearing a shirt with the logo from the hostel company I had spent the last several weeks working for; she had just come from Los Angeles, and was on her way back to China. Since Hawaii was a cheap one-way ticket from Los Angeles, it only made sense to make it a stop on her way back to Beijing, she explained.

What I was starting to find was not only how accessible Hawaii was from the West Coast, but also how it *could* serve as a jumping off point for someone heading to Japan, Taiwan, Australia—all at a much lower cost than one might expect. Travel hacks like this are some of the keen, albeit often overlooked, advantages of staying at hostels, and the more you hear of them, the more difficult it becomes *not* to pack everything up and jettison to some foreign country on a whim, since the ones who are doing it will tell you just how easy it is.

Encounters like these, both with the girl in the van and the one at the hostel, both of whom knew several people I did, back in the States, make for good stories;

but, more than that, they go to show how tightly-knit the hostel circuit can be, even if at times it might seem like the best well-kept secret around. It comes as little surprise, then, why certain people choose to make it a lifestyle, instead of just a way to get around.

Some people, like Chrissy, might get lucky and wind up staying at one of the more social or even upscale hostels right off the bat, and that is what shapes their perception of the industry. As optimal as that may be, it is not always possible. Being that it was her first time staying in a hostel, when Chrissy arranged to meet my brother and me—two complete strangers—one afternoon for a day of exploring the island, she was, naturally, skeptical.

"I wasn't about to tell my friends back home what I was up to today," Chrissy laughed, sitting in the backseat of the car my brother had borrowed from his roommate. "They would have *definitely* made me share my location, which I can understand. This sort of thing isn't exactly normal, back home."

But, even though staying at a hostel was a bit out of her wheelhouse, Chrissy went on to say that she was glad she didn't bail on her reservation before getting a chance to see what they were all about. The idea had crossed her mind, she admitted, the first night she showed up, once she realized just how many things she would be sharing with complete strangers. A hotel would have been more comfortable, she said, but the girls in her room had been *so nice*, and so the decision to stick around soon became pretty easy. That was how Chrissy wound up with us, watching from the backseat as the road gave way to sweeping views of the crashing waves of the ocean on our way up the coast of the island.

Since none of us had any serious obligations for the day, we cruised the island of Oahu, with my brother playing tour guide to show off the various nooks, iconic eateries, and hidden lookouts along the way. Together we cracked beers at Lanikai Beach, watched the sunset from China Walls, shared stories of our travels, and some insights on what life was like back home, having grown up in different regions of the country but within the same span of a few years from one another.

When we went our separate ways, Chrissy thanked my brother and me for our kindness and for not being creepy or weird.

SAN FRANCISCO, CA

In a city like San Francisco, it's impossible not to feel like there is something you're missing out on all the time. As with exploring any city through hostels, but especially the major ones, it's usually a good idea to consult the staff for the must-dos or places that are worth avoiding. Having spent two years in the city, Nikole was naturally the one I sought out for such advice. We had met in Santa Barbara, but now I was on her turf, so she sat me down after our interview over breakfast and pulled out a map of San Francisco, making circles on all of the iconic spots while not overlooking some of the hidden gems in the city.

It was because of my friend's advice that I found myself wandering through Golden Gate Park a few hours later before winding my way up Strawberry Hill to take in the sweeping views of the Golden Gate Bridge as well as the city itself, and then later staggering my way back to Chinatown, stopping through several funky eateries and interesting bookstores in the iconic Haight-Ashbury neighborhood. As optimal as it is to have solid recommendations, wearing the right shoes while touring San Francisco can be just as important.

Seeing the city start to come back to life—after being rocked by the pandemic—was nothing short of remarkable, yet hardly surprising as I carved my way through the hilly streets on foot, opting against any public transportation, partly to save a few dollars but also to *see* things instead of merely passing by them on some crowded bus or rail car. And even though the rebound in San Francisco had yet to take full effect, the signs were there that things *were* returning to normal. At the same time, though, it always seemed a bit preposterous to think that a city of San Francisco's caliber would *not* rebound and regain its footing, since there are few like it, and certain indelible characteristics will always make it special, and coveted by Americans and foreigners.

Being that North Beach was at one point a mecca for thinkers and artists of all sorts, I often found myself gravitating there on my visits, whether that was swinging through Vesuvio for a drink, perusing City Lights Books on a lazy Sunday, or drinking coffee at Cafe Trieste a few minutes after it opened. Especially as a writer, it became hard *not* to find the neighborhood endearing, knowing that the likes of Ginsberg, Watts, and even Coppola had also come to frequent those same haunts.

Sitting in a place like Cafe Trieste, moreover, and eavesdropping on the old heads who, I could only assume, had been coming there since the 70s, congregating over their same tables and bantering about baseball or bemoaning the local labor unions as they lazily did their crosswords, is just one of the many ways for one to get a glimpse at how things used to be, but perhaps, even more, small vantage points like that are an indicator of how some things in San Francisco will always stay the same, no matter how much else changes in the world around it.

20

Why we Stay, and how Some get Stuck

E ach stop on the map, however brief, has resonated for different reasons, which is, I believe, the beauty of travel. Surveying the depths of certain places to the lengths that I have, albeit while having a few strange or slightly uncomfortable situations along the way, would not have been possible had I opted for the comforts of a hotel room or decided to rent out someone's spare bedroom in one of these cities for a stretch, as I once did before discovering hostels.

Part of their draw for me has always been the price; as described in the dictionary, one of the key defining qualities of a hostel is its affordability. By traveling cheaply, there might then be a little extra money in the budget to see and feel many of the things that make a place so special or, in some instances, misunderstood. Part of what makes traveling anywhere new is being able to meet and connect with people from the places you *have not* been before, and have only heard about, and then *they* become the vessel through which you learn and better understand said place.

Meeting people, moreover, from all corners of the globe, and especially certain parts of *America*, can make you feel connected to those parts, even if you have never been or have only briefly passed through, because of how *they* might remind you of *someone else* that you know from there, and sometimes several others.

The portrait, then, of how *they* live, think, and feel, is slowly filled out; you might have the contours of a certain region or country figured out, but it's the people that color in the lines and add depth to that abstract piece of art one might call humanity.

In his red polyester tracksuit, Sam is someone who became a fascinating regional study. Within minutes of meeting him in Santa Barbara, I saw shades of my friend Eddie, who was born in a town just up the road from Sam, in Rhode Island. Even though they had rather different personalities, the little social cues, idiosyncrasies, and their affection for certain regional delicacies made me feel as if I already knew Sam quite well, because of Eddie.

Knowing his time at the hostel would be up eventually, and that the tight team working there would continue to splinter off with each subsequent departure, the only way to approach my friendship with Sam was with keen ears and a watchful eye, so that I could pick up on more of those little cues or file away a few of his slang terms, and so next time I found myself in close company with another Rhodey, I'd know which questions to skip and which ones might trigger some lengthy segue on 'dynamites' or what was going on with the regional hockey teams.

Like Eddie, some unspoken urge called Sam to leave that small town and see what life was like on the other side of the country—and now he was chasing the experience, that *thing*, even if that sometimes came with the lean times of stacking every dollar while still making sure there was enough to spare for his guilty pleasure of a 'two for one' hot dog deal from the local Sevy. Not ideal by most measures, especially in an affluent beach town like Santa Barbara, but the fear, the uncertainty, the difficulty of doing a lot with so little, however, is what made the challenge of it so fulfilling for my new friend, and even, I can only presume, addicting.

Just as well as living on a shoestring budget, the idea of being *comfortable* somewhere for a while can just as easily become uncomfortable for vagabonds or nomadic wanderers like myself, Sam, and countless others who did not find their way into this book. The struggle is, moreover, part of what makes the upshot so rewarding, even if that pinnacle, a realization of paradise or that idyllic way of living, is understood to be inherently fleeting as one sits in the sand, staring out over the ocean, thinking instead about not only what is next, but how to get there.

Having worked at more than half a dozen hostels across the United States, Sam had much to glean on about the lifestyle, and how such an approach to living can be wildly enriching, bouncing around cities and hostels like they're friend's couches, but also how it can also become, like anything else, stale, and suck one into certain ruts if they're not careful. Seeing that staleness can just as easily gnaw away at one's ambition and lead to breaking good, wholesome routines, only to supplant them with lazy habits, Sam was not shy to express that, for him, keeping things fresh was as important as finding somewhere worthwhile to stay for a while.

Finding ways to make it possible and follow through on that burning desire to shake things up can be difficult when you're chasing this *thing* on a lean budget. Through people like Sam, it was only reinforced to me, especially as a traveler, how necessary it is to have some resilience but also still channel one's zeal for the unknown, understanding that it's a chapter of life you'll never get back. So even if that means squeezing every penny or having to tact when the wind suddenly shifts, you might as well make the most of it, because the ride will be over before you know it.

Yet, if you stay long enough, especially as a volunteer, you might find that you're the last one standing. It can be a lonely feeling, which can seem foreign and incomprehensible in a place like this, especially given how wildly different the vibe might have been just last week. But it has happened to me, and only through that experience, I tried to warn Alex in Los Angeles, who was watching one staff member after another board planes, trains, buses, for somewhere else — and she was still hanging on. That tight-knit group of staff members that she had been a part of, at the beachside hostel that summer, was dwindling with each day, and it was starting to become obvious with each empty seat in the common room that the new aura of the hostel would take some time getting adjusted to.

Alex's crew had seized that distinct 'lightning in a bottle' that is so elusive but at times so palpable within a staff, or even amidst a wave of guests at a specific time; and yet, for as simplistic as the concept might seem — a collection of energies that come together at the right time, in one place — such a thing can be rather difficult to truly find in hostels, and even more difficult to maintain. Because the essence, the beauty of what makes being somewhere for a while, with the same people, and developing that kinship that can only be established through the peaks and lows of keeping a place like that upbeat and operational, is what makes it so heart-wrenching when the realization hits that the time is up and it's time for life to go back to normal, even if *that* no longer feels normal or in fact necessary.

As idyllic as it might be for everyone on staff to stay rooted, and truly establish that place as their home for more than a month or two at a time, the reality is that such a thing is not possible, given how not only people's needs change, but also how such a setup can start to impact the way one looks at it. Keeping it fresh is essential to keeping oneself fresh, and although you might hate to watch one of your new best friends suddenly leave, it's important to remember that it's the best thing for them.

So, eventually, you do have to say goodbye, which is as integral to the experience as saying hello. The next goodbye is never easier than the last, but there's something beautiful, still, in seeing that there is something to be emotional about—that means *it* worked, and it all went well enough to be disappointed about its ending, even if that can be abrupt sometimes or seem completely unfair.

It can be a lot to keep up with, and sometimes difficult to compartmentalize. All of the farewells, which are better phrased as 'see you soon' start to add up to where you realize you have a long list of people to see in different places, several of whom are off doing interesting things on another side of the planet, or simply the others who have started that new chapter in life they talked about on their way through the hostel. Even though you might not exactly be certain about the 'soon' part in 'see you soon,' it feels wrong *not* to keep up with them, at least every now and then.

The impermanence of it all is, rather, part of what makes the experience so enriching and wildly unique, even if the highs of a fun night out or a weekend jammed pack with new places can feel cruel once Monday morning rolls around or that plane has to take off. But getting caught up in the things you cannot control will only hold you back from having more experiences like the one you just had, especially in a place like this.

Closing Thoughts

Countless things about the industry, the lifestyle, the people, I am certain to have missed, and will likely remember once this book is published and put on the shelf somewhere, but rather than trying to expound any further on this strange and sometimes confounding, but yet wildly fulfilling way of living and traveling, I'd rather suggest that you try it out for yourself. You might be surprised by what you find.

www.ingramcontent.com/pod-product-compliance
Lightning Source LLC
Chambersburg PA
CBHW031457120626
46545CB00005B/1650